Progress in IS

More information about this series at http://www.springer.com/series/10440

Jörg Becker • Oleg Kozyrev • Eduard Babkin •
Victor Taratukhin • Natalia Aseeva
Editors

Emerging Trends in Information Systems

Recent Innovations, Results and Experiences

 Springer

Editors
Jörg Becker
ERCIS
University of Münster
Münster, Germany

Oleg Kozyrev
Higher School of Economics
National Research University
Nizhny Novgorod, Russia

Eduard Babkin
Higher School of Economics
National Research University
Nizhny Novgorod, Russia

Victor Taratukhin
University of Münster
Münster, Germany

Natalia Aseeva
Higher School of Economics
National Research University
Nizhny Novgorod, Russia

ISSN 2196-8705   ISSN 2196-8713 (electronic)
Progress in IS
ISBN 978-3-319-37051-4   ISBN 978-3-319-23929-3 (eBook)
DOI 10.1007/978-3-319-23929-3

Contents

IT-Support Within Facility Management in West- and Eastern Europe

Alexander Redlein and Michael Zobl

Abstract Since 2005 the Vienna University of Technology (TU Vienna) analyse the IT systems that are used to support Facility Management (FM) and Real Estate processes on a yearly basis. These studies show that most of the surveyed companies use standard software (ERP) rather than graphics-oriented software (CAFM) to cover FM processes and functions. The studies also analyse which business processes are covered by these systems, the reasons for implementing these systems and the benefits of the use of these IT systems. The research is based on the Mixed Method Approach and the Mixed Model Research.

Keywords Enterprise resource planning (ERP) • Computer aided facility management (CAFM) • Facility management (FM) • Mixed method research

1 Introduction

After salary and wages, expenditures for facility and real estate represent the largest part of the operating expenses for an organisation. Any improvement of cost effectiveness results in overall cost savings. Facility Management (FM) is a key function to support the core business of the organisation and can contribute to the success or the partial failure of an organisation's business [1]. According to different publications it is possible to save between 10 and 30 % of the costs of buildings through the use of FM. The European Norm EN 15221-1 defines FM as follows: "In general, all organisations, whether public or private, use buildings, assets and services (facility services) to support their primary activities. By coordinating these assets and services, using management skills and handling many changes in the organisation's environment, Facility Management influences the ability to act proactively and meet all its requirements. This is also done to optimize the costs and performance of assets and services" (EN 15221-1:2006). Over the past years the adoption of information technologies (IT) has affected property and facility management (FM). IT tools and methods allow control over the complexity

A. Redlein • M. Zobl (✉)
Vienna University of Technology, IFM, Wien 1040, Austria
e-mail: redlein@tuwien.ac.at

© Springer International Publishing Switzerland 2016
J. Becker et al. (eds.), *Emerging Trends in Information Systems*, Progress in IS,
DOI 10.1007/978-3-319-23929-3_1

of FM processes and services. Therefore, IT support becomes an important factor of the realization of FM [2].

Two IT systems that are used to support FM and Real Estate processes are ERP-systems and CAFM-systems. ERP (Enterprise Resource Planning) emerged as a complete business software system that enables companies to share common data and activities throughout the entire enterprise, automate and integrate the critical parts of its business processes and generate and access information in a real-time environment. The ERP system helps create re-energized organizations that are in a position to better serve costumers, empower employees, and drive greater business value [3]. ERP integrates key business and management functions and provides a view of the happenings in the company, in the areas of finance, human resources, manufacturing, asset management, production planning, sales and distribution etc. [4]. ERP systems provide the means for management to respond to the increasing business needs in more efficient and effective ways [5]. Most of these systems include functionality which supports day to day work of FM or Controlling, such as material management, project management, workflow, maintenance/repair, quality assurance and tenant management. Beside this support of the operative work, ERP systems also deliver data which are the basis for the work of the Facility Manager or support parts of FM processes, e.g. general accounting, cost accounting and controlling. FM processes may also support or provide data for ERP processes such as human resource management, asset management, maintenance and controlling [6]. CAFM (Computer Aided Facility Management) describes the support of FM processes and users by information technology (IT). It has been providing efficient IT tools for the mapping, evaluation and controlling of FM structures and processes [2]. This system usually includes a data and a drawing (CAD) component. It can be composed of several different software packages or it can describe a single software system. It is a high-tech tool used by facility professionals to track and manage virtually any facility-related asset. It provides managers and decision makers with the ability to analyse the effective use of space more readily than ever [7]. The basic function of CAFM tools is to manage basic building data and space information. Modern systems work on a graphical basis and include drawings. CAFM tools also provide a lot of interfaces to other systems, such as telephone systems, security systems and business software. These tools integrate graphic and database data to provide process support for special FM functions such as: space management, move management, cleaning management, inventory management, access control and key management, FM related personnel management, real estate management and building maintenance management. To provide this process support an integration of graphic and alphanumeric data is needed. One source of the data are digital drawings of the building. Therefore in the first step digital drawings of the buildings are imported into these tools. Besides this building related data (area, volume etc.), other data, such as cost related data are needed within a CAFM tool. These data origin from other IT systems. These data must be available within the CAFM tools. In the next step to bring together these different data source links must be established. At the minimum this link for the cost related data can be established by defining the organisational unit which uses each room of a building. If this is done automatically, the area, volume and other attributes of a room or building are related with the organisational unit, or rather its cost centre. By using reports all building related data, which are necessary for calculating benchmarks, can be extracted [6]. Benefits are: the advantage of sharing data with other departments, faster processing time, cost savings, reduced crisis management, reduced personnel, better control of information and improvement of processes [8]. The decision for the CAFM software should be based on the needed functionality, flexibility, the possible links to other systems and the costumer's and supplier's company strategy. So, there is a need for process integration of CAFM and ERP systems within FM [6].

Since 2005 the Vienna University of Technology (TU Vienna) analyze the demand side of FM on a yearly basis in different European countries such as Austria, Germany, Bulgaria, Romania and Turkey. The companies were selected randomly. The researches have been based on (standardized) questionnaire survey. This paper presents some results of the surveys in the area of FM performed by the Vienna University of Technology. It shows the use of a CAFM and an ERP system within FM, the business processes covered with these systems and the benefits of the use of these systems.

2 Methodology

The authors used the research method "Mixed Research". The Mixed Research is a general type of research in which quantitative and qualitative research methods, techniques, or other paradigm characteristics are mixed in an overall study. The two major types are the Mixed Method Research/Approach and the Mixed Model Research [9]. The Mixed Method Research combines quantitative surveys with qualitative data collection methods e.g. personal interviews, expert groups, focus groups with professionals and content analysis [10]. Its logic of inquiry includes the use of induction (discovery of patterns), deduction (testing of theories and hypotheses) and abduction (uncovering and relying on the best of a set of explanations for understanding one's results). The goal is to draw from the strengths and minimize the weaknesses of the quantitative and qualitative research methods in single research studies or across studies [11].

Based on the Mixed Method Research, the studies include quantitative and qualitative research phases. The first step was to analyse and validate the existing data and the results of the former surveys. In addition, qualitative surveys (literature review, expert interviews etc.) were used to analyse problems, define additional parameters and improve the questionnaire. Then new hypotheses were set up. Based on the new hypotheses, a new questionnaire was set up and the survey was carried out. An extended ex post office analysis of the existing profit and loss reports and balance sheet was performed. The main goal of this step was to provide more accurate data. An indexation of the respective years should verify that the results are comparable [12]. Also the Mixed Model Research was used. The qualitative and quantitative approaches are mixed within a stage of a study or across two of the stages of the research process [9]. The questionnaire included summated rating scales (quantitative data collection) and open-ended questions (qualitative data collection). The questionnaire was subdivided into the parts: companies in general (e.g. questions about the industry of the company, turnover, number of employees), FM organisation (questions about the availability of a FM department, number of employees etc.), value added (e.g. cost drivers and savings through the introduction of FM, increase in productivity through the use of FM), IT support (used IT systems, areas of IT support etc.) and sustainability (e.g. what contribution can FM deliver to sustainability). Depending on the answers there are up to about 40 questions. The population for the survey were the Top 500 companies in the different countries (ranking is sales driven). Interviewees were the Facility Managers themselves or the persons responsible for all FM tasks according to the European Norm EN 15221-1. Tools for the survey were phone, personal face-to-face interviews and/or E-Mail. The phone interviews with the Facility Managers respectively the persons responsible for all FM tasks of the different companies were carried out by one researcher, thus the manner of questioning was always the same. This was done to secure the data quality. The data (answers) were entered in a MS Access databases and afterwards exported into statistical programs and analyzed and evaluated. SPSS (IBM SPSS Predictive Analytics Software) is used to evaluate the data and to set up statistical models.

This paper presents some first results of the quantitative part of the surveys in Austria 2012 and Romania 2013 especially IT Support within FM.

3 Results

CAFM and ERP systems deliver data which are the basis for the work of the Facility Manager or support parts of the FM processes. Figure 1 shows that only 36 % of the surveyed companies in Austria 2012 (N = 82) and Romania 2013 (N = 16) used a CAFM system and 71 % (Austria 2012) respectively 80 % (Romania 2013) used an ERP system. So, most of the surveyed companies use standard software (ERP) rather than graphics-oriented software (CAFM) to cover FM processes and functions.

The ERP tools are supposed to support the administrative work, but also core processes within organisations. They provide functions like financial accounting and bookkeeping, asset management, cost accounting, material management, controlling, human resource management and quality management. Figure 2 shows the FM processes covered with the ERP system sorted by the number of mentions. The most mentioned FM processes covered with the ERP system are: cost accounting and controlling, financial accounting, material management, asset accounting, human resource management, distribution, business processes, production, maintenance/repair and organisation. These tools include functionality which supports the work of FM Services or Controlling. Besides this support of the operative work,

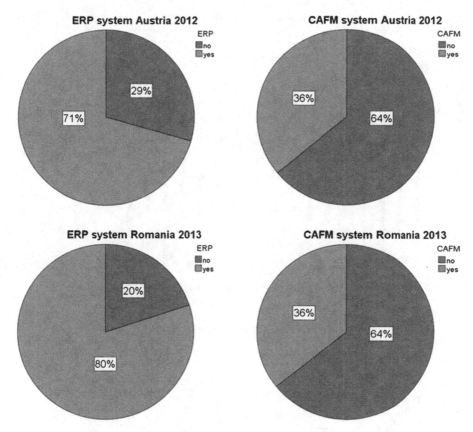

Fig. 1 ERP and CAFM system (Austria 2012 and Romania 2013)

ERP systems also deliver data which are the basis for the work of Facility Manager or support parts of FM processes. For example the financial transactions of the financial accounting have an impact on cost accounting which can be used to provide cost transparency. This means to show the "users" the real cost of the usage of facilities. The result of cost accounting is one information basis for management information systems; others are facility usage information and user satisfaction [6].

The reasons for implementing an ERP system are: consistent documentation, modernisation, facilitate handling, quick analysis, increase in productivity, cost saving and utilization of synergies. Organizations view ERP-enabled standardization as a vital means to integrate dispersed organizational systems, provide a seamless access to information organization-wide and make informed decisions on strategic and daily business matters [13].

CAFM tools are made for handling building related data. It ranges from a simple space management tool to a range of applications such as: maintenance and operations, facility budgeting and accounting, construction and project

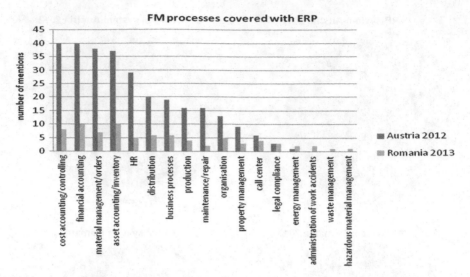

Fig. 2 FM processes covered with the ERP system (Austria 2012 and Romania 2013)

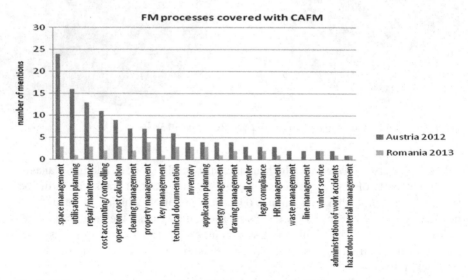

Fig. 3 FM processes covered with the CAFM system (Austria 2012 and Romania 2013)

management, space inventory and management, architectural and interior planning, lease and property management and furniture and equipment management [8]. The CAFM tools integrate graphic and database data to provide process support for special FM functions. Figure 3 shows the FM processes covered with the CAFM system sorted by the number of mentions. The most mentioned processes covered are: space management, utilisation planning, maintenance/repair, cost accounting/ controlling, operation cost calculation, cleaning management, property management, key management, technical documentation, inventory and application planning. These tools support day to day facilities operations, from master planning to project design and budgeting, from construction to lease management. Such technology increases accuracy through data validation, but remains flexible in reporting and inquiry. CAFM tools are intended to reduce management costs by creating a central and comprehensive resource for facilities information [7].

The reasons for implementing a CAFM system are: facilitate handling, consistent documentation, cost saving, utilization of synergies, quick analysis, increase in productivity, control of processes, reduce complexity, ensure data security and achieve transparency. Overall, the implementation of a CAFM system supports and improves the FM processes. It represents the support and realization of the FM concept throughout the entire life cycle of a real estate property [2].

As mentioned before, one reason for implementing an ERP and/or CAFM system is to achieve an increase in productivity. ERP systems are beneficial in providing support for all variations of best business practices with a view towards enhancing productivity and in empowering the costumer to modify the implemented business processes to suit their needs [13]. ERP systems can integrate business applications using real-time information. Therefore, ERP systems provide the means for management to respond to the increasing business needs in more effective and efficient ways. The benefits of ERP systems are seen as the production of real-time data shared across the organization and the integration and automation of business processes [5]. Through fast and accurate information sharing, process improvement, and production and financial flexibility, organizations can respond to the market quickly and proactively thereby having a positive impact on financial and non-financial performance measures [14]. The potentials of the implementation of a CAFM system lie in the improvement of processes and their integration as well as human factor [2]. The benefits realised from a CAFM system are: time savings, accuracy of data validation, form standardisation, creation of a flexible data set for reporting and analysis [7]. Others are to achieve transparency of information, direct access to data and an improvement in planning performance and quality [15]. Process optimization, time savings, distribution of forms with existing infrastructure and standard software, integration of applications, easy maintenance of database and reorganization through the use of an ERP and/or CAFM system can lead to an increase in productivity.

To analyze the correlation between the use of an ERP respectively a CAFM system and the increase in productivity an equivalent test was used. The equivalent test was used for comparing the average performance of two groups to verify if there is a difference between two populations on the basis of the random sample form these populations [16]. Because of the non-normal distribution of the data the authors used the Wilcoxon Test to verify if there is a difference between two populations. The Wilcoxon Test can be used as a nonparametric replacement or substitute for the t-Test. Most nonparametric methods use statistics, such as the median, that are resistant to outliers and skewness. The null hypothesis (H_0) states that, in the population, the two medians are equal, which means that there is "no effect". The alternative hypothesis (H_1) states that there is a difference between the two medians, which means that there is an "effect". A statistical test is said to show significance if the p-value is less than the significance level ($p < 0.05$). Then the null hypothesis is rejected and the alternative hypothesis is supported [17].

The hypothesis is that a use of an ERP system will generate better data, process optimization and higher effectiveness and efficiency in operations and therefore will increase the productivity respectively will tend to more areas of increased productivity. The data for Austria 2012 and Romania 2013 will be considered.

The null hypothesis is:

H_0 = Companies with an ERP system have the same number of areas of increased productivity as companies without an ERP system.

The alternative hypothesis is:

H_1 = Companies with an ERP system tend to have more areas of increased productivity than companies without a similarly software.

Tested Variable:

Areas of Productivity (number of nominations, e.g. maintenance/repair, infrastructure, administration)

Variable of Grouping:

Using of an ERP system (yes/no) for Austria 2012 and Romania 2013 (Table 1)

The significant result ($p < 0.05$) of the Wilcoxon Test shows that there is a difference between the two medians, which means that there is an effect (H_1). Companies which cover FM processes with an ERP system tend to have more areas of increased productivity than companies without a similarly software. That means companies which are using an ERP system tend to nominate more areas of productivity than companies without an ERP system. This result confirms that the use of an ERP system (possible) gains in increase of productivity. Process optimization, reduction in working capitals, real-time access to operating and financial data, integration of applications, easy maintenance of database and reorganization through the use of an ERP system can lead to an increase in productivity.

Another hypothesis is that a use of a CAFM software will generate better data, improvement in planning performance and quality etc. and therefore optimize the FM processes. This will lead to an increase in productivity.

Table 1 Number of areas of productivity—ERP system (Austria 2012 and Romania 2013)		Austria 2012 and Romania 2013	
		ERP system	Without an ERP system
	N	41	16
	Mean[a]	1.34	0.69
	Median[a]	1.00	0.50
	Std. deviation	1.425	0.793
	p-value	→ Validated with 0.006964 → H1	

[a]Areas of productivity (number of mentions)

Table 2 Number of areas of productivity—CAFM system (Austria 2012 and Romania 2013)

	Austria 2012 and Romania 2013	
	CAFM system	Without a CAFM system
N	20	37
Mean[a]	2.00	0.92
Median[a]	1.50	1.00
Std. deviation	2.248	0.924
p-value	→Validated with 0.006964 → H1	

[a]Areas of productivity (number of mentions)

The null hypothesis is:

H_0 = Companies with CAFM software have the same number of areas of increased productivity as companies without CAFM software.

The alternative hypothesis is:

H_1 = Companies with CAFM software tend to have more areas of increased productivity than companies without a similarly software.

Tested Variable:

Areas of Productivity (number of nominations, e.g. maintenance/repair, infrastructure, administration)

Variable of Grouping:

Using of an CAFM system (yes/no) for Austria 2012 and Romania 2013 (Table 2)

Companies which are using CAFM software tend to nominate more areas of productivity than companies without CAFM. The result is significant (p-value < 0.05), which means that the alternative hypothesis (H_1) is supported.

Companies with an ERP and/or a CAFM software tend toward a higher number of areas of productivity. In addition, companies with these tools tend towards a higher number of cost drivers (at the introduction phase) because of the need to collect and maintain data. Not only the tool itself but also the training of the employees causes costs. But, if successfully implemented, these tools increase the productivity of FM respectively facility services and therefore the productivity of the company. A better database increases the simplification of the operational procedures of FM. Due to the introduction of these tools, rapid data access and evaluation is possible. This enables decisions that are more precise. Better data generation, process optimization and higher effectiveness and efficiency in operations through the use of these tools will increase the productivity.

4   Conclusion

Most of the ERP and CAFM systems include functionality which supports the daily work of Facility Management Services. FM processes covered with these systems are e.g., space management, cost accounting/controlling, utilization planning, maintenance/repair, financial accounting and material management. Most of the surveyed companies use standard software (ERP) rather than graphics-oriented software (CAFM) to cover FM processes and functions. When successfully implemented, the potential benefits include declines in inventory, reductions in working capital, process optimization, increase in productivity and cost savings. These benefits are all critical for the survival and growth of many companies.

References

1. Chotipanich, S. (2004). Positioning facility management. *Facilities, 22*(13/14), 364–372.
2. Madritsch, T., & May, M. (2009). Successful IT implementation in facility management. *Facilities, 27*(11/12), 429–444.
3. Willis, T., & Willis-Brown, A. (2002). Extending the value of ERP. *Industrial Management & Data Systems, 102*(1), 35–38.
4. Kakouris, A. P., & Polychronopoulos, G. (2005). Enterprise resource planning (ERP) system: An effective tool for production management. *Management Research News, 28*(6), 66–78.
5. Spathis, C., & Constantinides, S. (2003). The usefulness of ERP systems for effective management. *Industrial Management & Data Systems, 103*(9), 677–685.
6. Redlein, A. (2004). *Facility management: Business process integration*. Hamburg: Diplomica GmbH.
7. Keller, J., & Keller, C. (2004). Bringing strategic efficacy to facility management through CAFM tools. *Journal of Facilities Management, 3*(2), 125–144.
8. Elmualim, A., & Pelumi-Johnson, A. (2009). Application of computer-aided facilities management (CAFM) for intelligent buildings operation. *Facilities, 27*(11/12), 421–428.
9. Johnson, R. B., & Christensen, L. (2007). *Educational research: Quantitative, qualitative and mixed approaches* (3rd ed.). Thousand Oaks: Sage.
10. Jensen, P. A., van der Voordt, T., Coenen, C., von Felten, D., Lindholm, A.-L., et al. (2012). In search for the added value of FM: What we know and what we need to learn. *Facilities, 30*(5), 199–217.
11. Johnson, R. B., & Onwuegbuzie, A. J. (2004). Mixed method research: A research paradigm whose time has come. *Educational Researcher, 33*(7), 14–26.
12. Redlein, A., & Sustr, F. (2008). *Economic effective implementation of FM*. Research paper, TU Wien.
13. Al-Mashari, M. (2003). Enterprise resource planning (ERP) systems: A research agenda. *Industrial Management & Data Systems, 103*(1), 22–27.
14. Hassab-Elnaby, H., Hwang, W., & Vonderembse, M. (2012). The impact of ERP implementation on organizational capabilities and firm performance. *Benchmarking: An International Journal, 19*(4/5), 618–633.
15. Abel, J., & Lennerts, K. (2005). Where does CAFM really help? Current fields of application and future tends according to system user. In *Proceedings of CIB W78's 22nd international conference on information technology in construction*, CIB Publication 304, The Westin Bellevue, Dresden, Germany, June 19–21, 2005.
16. Dodge, Y. (2008). *The concise encyclopedia of statistics*. Berlin: Springer.
17. Kinnear, P., & Gray, C. (2008). *SPSS 15 made simple*. New York: Psychology Press.

Continuous Acquisition and Life-Cycle Support (CALS) Simulation Models on the Basis of the ERP and CAD Technologies Integration

Victor M. Kureichik, Vladimir V. Kureichik, Victor V. Taratukhin, Yury A. Kravchenko, and Anna I. Khlebnikova

Abstract In present article an intellectual data analysis and simulation modeling methods were used for management of information flows of manufacturing enterprise on the basis of ERP (Enterprise Resource Planning) and CAD (Computer-aided design) systems. CALS-simulation model on the basis of Petri nets as an integration tool of the industrial automated systems in a uniform multifunctional business processes control system is designed. Data mining methods development for effective support of decision-making of steady meta-structures of logical data patterns identification are also investigated. The conceptual scheme of evolutionary modeling methods integration for intellectual data analysis of business processes management is developed.

Keywords ERP • CALS • CAD • Data mining • Petri nets • Decision support system (DSS)

1 Introduction

Nowadays, modern enterprises are faced a problem of a reliable control over a high volume of diverse data stored and used in the various information systems for information support of products during their life cycle.

The main purpose of research is creation of effective models simulation of business processes management in the conditions of uncertainty. Existence of uncertainty complicates the forecast of information flows stability and makes it impossible to create models on the basis of analytical expressions. Therefore intellectual data analysis methods application and CALS (Continuous Acquisition

V.M. Kureichik • V.V. Kureichik • Y.A. Kravchenko (✉) • A.I. Khlebnikova
Southern Federal University, Rostov-on-Don, Russia
e-mail: krav-jura@yandex.ru

V.V. Taratukhin
University of Muenster - ERCIS, Leonardo Campus 3, Münster 48149, Germany

© Springer International Publishing Switzerland 2016
J. Becker et al. (eds.), *Emerging Trends in Information Systems*, Progress in IS,
DOI 10.1007/978-3-319-23929-3_2

and Life-cycle Support)-technologies for an assessment of efficiency of ERP modules integration with external systems, on the example of CAD is expedient [1].

ERP (Enterprise Resources Planning) built on the basis of CALS technology help to solve this problem [2].

CALS technologies serve as integration tool of industrial multi-functional system. The purpose of integration of the automated systems of design and management is improvement of efficiency of design and usage of the complicated industrial systems by means of their effective interaction [3].

Key component of information integration is the PDM (Product Data Management) system—technology of management of complete product lifecycle data.

The main objective of PDM-technology is making information processes more transparent and controllable. The main method applied is increase of availability of data for all participants of product lifecycle. It requires integration of product's data in logically uniform information model.

The simulation modelling method is an essential part of automation allowing improvement of design and research of complex systems.

2 Simulation Model Design

The typical CAD architecture separately allocates the simulation block from other functional parts. Peculiarity of applied systems like CAD is integrity of design technology and the automated system:

- Methods and techniques used in the design organization influence on methods realized CAD;
- CAD functionality influences methods which are used by the design organization.

Introduction of simulation block into structure of CAD allows passing to new qualitative level of design. Quality of design is reached at the expense of possibility of more complex challenges solution and at the expense of increase in extent of same type design decisions making. At increase in power of a set of considered alternatives the engineer can use an identical technique [4]. Therefore he can apply the same technique. Extent of processes proceeding typing at design influences the cost of all process of development. According to the experts design cost owing to typing of the project can decrease by 3.3 times.

The constant increase in arrays of processed information results in need of processes intellectualization of the automated industrial design, thus one of the central tasks is creation of effective solution of problems of intellectual knowledge extraction. The problem of uncertainty is a component of a problem of complex systems solution state identification and forecasting. The model of complex system can't be based on the principles of the analysis as it will be inadequate to studied system as at division of system into compound components its certain properties are lost. Therefore detection of the hidden regularities between variables characterizing behavior of studied dynamic systems is an actual problem of the intellectual data analysis. Integration of the existing Data mining methods (DM) and Deep data mining (DDM) with the newest perspective directions of development of evolutionary modeling methods will allow to increase efficiency of procedures of forecasting, classification, clustering, association and other types of logical regularities in data.

3 Main Problems and Directions of Their Decision

Researches in the field of knowledge extraction are directed on the solution of information intellectual systems fundamental problems:

- Ranging, segmentation, forecasting, identification and identification of associations and exceptions in studied factors of complex dynamic systems design
- Developing the principles of the intellectual data analysis (Data mining), connected with carrying out complex theoretical researches in the field of evolutionary modelling

The problem of creation of theoretical models, methods and algorithms of the intellectual data analysis in the conditions of uncertainty, on the basis of integration of methods of evolutionary modelling, makes the important direction of researches within the specified problem.

Development and research of the fundamental principles of application of neural network technologies are also necessary for creation of new algorithms of definition of the main types of regularities in Data mining [5]. A certain attention should be paid to modernization and integration of means of increase of reasoning systems efficiency and subject-oriented analytical systems on the basis of genetic algorithms application and artificial neural networks. Important research problem is possibility of new technologies development of metastructures identification of logical regularities in data.

4 Development of Knowledge Discovery Methods in Conditions of Uncertainty

Development of the theory and the principles of creation of intellectual knowledge discovery in databases (KDD) in uncertain conditions have to be carried out on the basis of a combination of self-learning, self-organization, genetic search and neural networks that will allow to break a barrier of a local optimum. Application of evolutionary modelling technologies and artificial intelligence will allow increasing efficiency of search of useful information in a priori data. Optimization of data preparation procedures, choice of informative attributes and data cleaning will allow improving and accelerating processes of the further analysis by Data mining methods.

The conceptual solution scheme of the considered problems is development of the new principles of multidimensional extrapolation of conditions of complex dynamic systems can be carried out on the basis of strategy of the combined search of logical regularities of studied factors—combinations of different types of neural networks and genetic search.

The greatest interest is represented by development of new methods of forecasting on the basis of integration of properties of prototypes development by dynamic and complex neural networks. As well as methods of parameters forecasting of a condition of object generalization on prevalence and similarity with use of case based reasoning (CBR) models with expanded functionality in the direction of creation of models and the rules generalizing the previous experience. For this purpose it is possible to carry out integration of reasoning systems with the problem-oriented analytical systems (POAS), since the first—effectively predict behavior of dynamic systems on the basis of analogies, but don't create models, and the second—on the opposite, have the necessary device of empirical modelling.

Expediency of use of neural network systems for forecasting of properties of such objects is caused by specific properties of the neural networks (NN):

– Ability of the operational multiple parameter analysis;
– Tolerance to a lack of aprioristic information on predicted object dynamics;
– Possibility of the data processing, presented in different types of scales;
– Ability of identification of implicit analogies of precedents of the supervision protocol;
– Preservation of the properties at destruction of casually chosen part of neural network, that causes high reliability of a network;
– Ability to self-learn;
– Possibility of the events forecasting that weren't observed earlier in learning selection.

Neural networks properties are defined by its architecture, and also set of synaptic connections and neurons characteristics. Predictive neural network model has to be capable not only continuously process a large number of parameters of system, factors of an expected background, but also to consider diverse information on current and planned modes of object functioning [6]. The neural network system of forecasting, in turn, has to consider information on system work logic, reliability of its elements, as well as expert information.

Dynamic neural networks have opportunities for modelling of intellectual functions. Recognition systems on the basis of static neural networks are capable to approximate complex dividing surfaces in attribute space and to distinguish the hidden dependences.

Thus, at the heart of a neural network method of expeditious forecasting for formation of a prototype it is necessary to use abilities of complex neural networks, as the main instrument of extrapolation in attributes space not observed before a situation.

The main lack of multilayered neural networks that is seriously limiting their practical application is slow convergence [7]. For convergence acceleration it is necessary besides development of effective algorithms of the return distribution, embedding in a structure knowledge network of research object and preliminary learning to apply hybrid networks in which neural networks contact the structures of received forecasting on the basis of other technologies, i.e. conclusions are drawn on the basis of other evolutionary methods, and the membership functions of accessory are arranged with use of neural networks learning algorithms [8].

One of the perspective directions of development of similar systems is inclusion of the genetic algorithms (GA) in process of neural networks learning [9]. GA is used as procedure for network learning since application of back propagation algorithm significantly complicates learning procedure. Moreover, GA allows adjusting a neuro-controller when giving on its input the output coordinate of an object on the current and previous steps [10]. The combination of two perspective computing technologies—genetic algorithms and artificial neural networks—allows solving effectively a problem of forecasting of dynamic system behavior within an evolutionary paradigm.

Having generalized all offered principles of the intellectual data analysis methods development, it is possible to offer the following decision-making support system structure on a basis of Data mining technologies (Fig. 1).

Use of simulation modelling allows examination process simplifying of the received CAD decisions. Transparency of examination allows involving investors in project financing that in conditions when the project cost of design can reach hundreds and thousand dollars is a necessary condition of implementation of the project [11]. Besides, use of the simulation module in the course of carrying out examination of projects reduces examination time.

At simulation modelling of complex dynamic systems on the basis of Petri's nets set entrance flows of demands and define the corresponding system reaction. Output parameters calculated by processing of the statistics saved up at modelling [12].

Other approach of Petri's networks usage for the analysis of complex systems is also possible. It isn't connected with processes simulation and based on research of such properties of Petri's networks, as boundary, safe, terminal, live.

Simulating in Petri's networks is carried out at event level. Performance of event model in Petri's networks describes system behavior. Performance results analysis

Fig. 1 Decision-making
support system structure

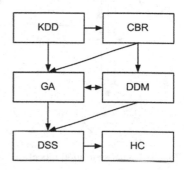

can tell what conditions the system stayed or didn't stay and what conditions aren't achievable [13].

Petri's network is represented as four <P, T, I, O>; where P and T—final sets of places and transitions, I and O—sets of input and output functions. In other words Petri net is directed bipartite graph in which the places—nodes signified by circles, and transitions, signified by bars; I functions—arc directed from places to transitions, and functions O—the arches directed from transitions to places [14].

As well as in systems of mass service, in Petri nets objects of two types are entered: dynamic which are represented by tokens (markers) in places, and static which nodes of Petri net correspond [15].

Distribution of markers on places called marking. Markers can move to networks. Each change of marking call an event, and each event is connected with a certain transition. It is considered that events occur instantly and asynchronously when performing some conditions.

To each condition in Petri net a certain place corresponds. Commit event corresponds operation (excitement or start) transition, in which markers from input positions of the markers in the input of this transition are moved to output positions. The sequence of events forms modelled process.

As an example, we will construct by means of Petri net the integrated simulation model of system functioning at integration level of design in CAD (Fig. 2).

Process of design begins with specification (S) discussion by interested persons of P1 and P2, in these places there are markers. According to rules of operation of transition to Petri nets, there is an operation of transition of T1. As a result, markers from positions of P1 and P2 passes to the following position P3, there is a specification on product design.

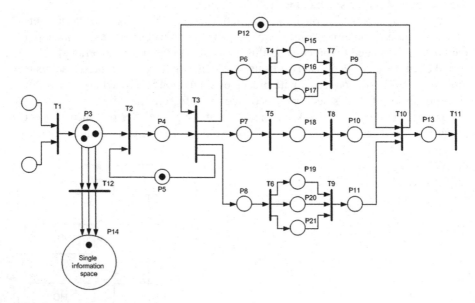

Fig. 2 CALS-simulation model

In Petri net there is such parameter as limitation (or K-limitation) if the number of tags in any position of a network can't exceed life-cycle's value design of the automated systems definition Limitation of all positions is equal in this network K1, except a position P3 in which this parameter is equal 3. Necessary data accumulates in a place P3 which in this case is PDM system distributing and operating data. Transition of T12 to a position P14 works if the quantity of markers in a place P3 reached maximum and T2 transition is closed. The place P14 imitates possibilities of the uniform information space (UIS) of the enterprise and markers (S) arrive on processing in similar divisions of design. Transition of T2 works in the presence of a marker in a place P5, showing that the place P4, is free for acceptance of a marker of S from a place P3. The place P4 is the beginning of process of system integration design. Transition of T3 works if in a place P12 there is a marker regulating load of this department by design work.

Places P6, P7, P8—indicate the main directions of conducted researches:

P6—define computer architecture
P15—functions identification
P16—functions division on hardware and software
P17—list of commands determination
P7—block diagram development
P18— quality options assessment
P8—modules requirements specification
P19—modules functions definition
P20—data format development
P21—base elements items

Transitions of T4, T5, T6 work when in places P6, P7, P8 there are markers of continuation of design process. Transitions of T7, T8, T9 work when markers are in the previous places. In each position of process of design temporary delays connected with need of the synchronization of data transmission are possible. In Petri's networks it is described as model time, to model not only sequence of events, but also their binding at the right time. Transition of T10 is the end of integration system design. It works at the moment when in all places P9, P10, P11 markers that testify the end of development task appear. At operation of this transition the marker passes to places: P12, P13 meaning readiness for a new cycle of integration system design. Further, works T11 transition, then developed specification (S) arrives in PDM system.

Processes management functions in PDM-system are intended for control ways of data change and creation. Process management concerns a product life-cycle support procedures and their influence on product data. It is possible to distinguish three main groups from its functions:

1. Work management (consider what happens to data when someone works over them).
2. Work flow management (operate data exchange).

3. Work logging (trace all events and actions, which occur when performing the first two groups of functions during all history of the project).

5 Conclusions

CALS-technologies can effectively manage information flows, creating and using a single information space. Major barrier to the widespread use of this approach in CAD and ERP is the problem of ever-increasing amounts of data being analyzed. Integration of CALS-technologies and data mining approaches will greatly improve multipurpose decision support systems (DSS).

The direction of evolutionary modeling applications for creation of new theoretical provisions, methods and algorithms of definition of a number of the main types of regularities of Data mining—classification, a clustering, association and sequence in the conditions of selections, insufficient aprioristic information on correlations between studied factors, nonlinear dependences, noisy and incomplete data is perspective.

For the purpose of efficiency increase of evolutionary search process it is necessary to develop and theoretically prove model of integration of subject-oriented analytical systems and genetic algorithms, for the purpose of an exception of unproductive branches of evolution. The subsequent inspection of the received models on adequacy can be made by development of multilevel neural network architecture of received systems models test.

References

1. Becker, Y., Vilkov, L., Taratukhin, V., Kugeler, M., & Rozemann, M. (2007). *Management of processes* (p. 112). Moscow: Eksmo.
2. Andreychikov, A., & Andreychikova, O. (2004). *Intellectual information system* (p. 312). Moscow: Finance and Statistics.
3. Norenkov, I. P., & Kuzmik, P. K. (2002). *Information support of the knowledge-intensive products* (p. 83). Moscow: CALS Technologies, MGTU of AD Bauman.
4. Kureichik, V. V., Kureichik, V. M., Kovalev, S. M., & Sokolov, S. V. (2011). Optical fuzzy logic systems in problems of adaptive simulation of weakly formalized processes. *Journal of Computer and Systems Sciences International, 50*(3), 462–471.
5. Fu, Y. (2001). Distributed data mining: An overview. In *IEEE TCDP newsletter*.
6. Dimou, Ch., Symeonidis Andreas, L., & Mitkas Pericles, A. (2007). Evaluating knowledge intensive multi-agent systems. In *Second international workshop, AIS-ADM, proceedings* (pp. 74–87). Berlin: Springer.
7. Lotfi, A., & Zadeh. (2002). In quest of performance metrics for intelligent systems a challenge that cannot be met with existing methods. In *Proceedings of the third international workshop on performance metrics for intelligent systems (PERMIS)*.
8. Kravchenko, Y. A., & Kureichik, V. V. (2013). Bioinspired algorithm applied to solve the travelling salesman problem. *World Applied Sciences Journal, 22*(12), 1789–1797.

9. Colodro, F., & Torralba, A. (1996). Cellular neuro-fuzzy networks (CNFNs), a new class of cellular networks. In *Proceedings of 5th IEEE international conference fuzzy systems* (Vol. 1, pp. 517–521) September 8–11.
10. Symeonidis, A. L., & Mitkas, P. A. (2005). *Agent intelligence through data mining.* New York: Springer.
11. Kitchenham, B. A. (1996). Evaluating software engineering methods. Part 2: Selecting an appropriate evaluation method technical criteria. *SIGSOFT Software Engineering Notes, 21* (2), 11–15.
12. Lin, C. T., Chang, C. L., & Cheng, W. C. (2004). A recurrent fuzzy neural network system with automatic structure and template learning. *IEEE Transactions on Circuits and Systems I: Regular Papers, 51*(5), 1024–1035.
13. Shih, T. K. (2000). Evolution of mobile agents. In *Proceedings of the first International workshop on performance metrics for intelligent systems (PERMIS).*
14. Zaporozhets, D. Y., Zaruba, D. V., & Kureichik, V. V. (2013). Hybrid bionic algorithms for solving problems of parametric optimization. *World Applied Sciences Journal, 23*(8), 1032–1036.
15. Kureichik, V. M., Lebedev, B. K., & Lebedev, V. B. (2013). VLSI floorplanning based on the integration of adaptive search models. *Journal of Computer and Systems Sciences International, 52*(1), 80–96.

The Process-Oriented Approach
for Designing a Project Management System

I.V. Abramov, I.V. Illarionov, and M.G. Matveev

Abstract The purpose of this paper is to demonstrate the advantages of the process approach as a uniform methodology for synthesizing an enterprise management system, and also the possibility to use this approach for designing a project management system.

Keywords Project management system • Enterprise management system • Process approach

1 Introduction

Improving efficiency and effectiveness of organizational management has always been one of the central problems for any organization. Management is considered efficient when the organization succeeds in achieving certain objectives through its operational and project activities. Operational activity of a mature organization is traditionally seen as a set, repetitive, and strongly regulated business process [1]. Project work, on the contrary, is usually a unique process, loosely controlled and limited in time [2]. What operational and project activities have in common, is that they both require a management system. By management we will understand a multistep process with negative feedback, aimed at reaching the set goal. To synthesize an organizational management system, it is necessary to create an organizational structure, develop regulations for the divisions and job descriptions for the employees.

One of the effective ways to solve this problem is the process approach [1, 3]. Within this approach, first, a Balanced Scorecard is designed with two types of target performance indicators: strategic performance indicators and process performance indicators. The latter can be reached through special processes (projects), while the first—through the whole operation of the organization (operational activity).

The process approach is successfully applied in business management systems such as Workflow management systems and Enterprise Resource Planning (ERP). Within this approach, first the organization's business process models, including management process models, are developed and analysed. Then it is necessary to

I.V. Abramov • I.V. Illarionov • M.G. Matveev (✉)
Voronezh State University, Voronezh, Russia
e-mail: mgmatveev@yandex.ru

© Springer International Publishing Switzerland 2016   21
J. Becker et al. (eds.), *Emerging Trends in Information Systems*, Progress in IS,
DOI 10.1007/978-3-319-23929-3_3

design the organizational structure of the operational activity, set the regulations and ensure the monitoring of the process. Management processes provide for the development of such business process parameters and structures that will ensure the achievement of the set indicators. We will further refer to operational activity management as an operational management.

It is not possible to apply operational management to separate projects, as they are unique and unpredictable. But it is possible, and even necessary, to manage the project lifecycle processes, as they can be unified, which is proved by various methodologies and standards of project management, as in [4]. The said processes can be repeated not only in different projects, but also within the same lifecycle, when returning to previous stages for adjustments. In this case, the object of management are the project lifecycle processes, and the management objective is to choose such parameters and structures for these processes that will provide for the goal implementation. We will further refer to such type of management as project management. The structure of the integrated enterprise management system combining both operational management system (OMS) and project management system (PMS) is represented in Fig. 1.

Management of both operational and project activities is performed within the organizational structure. Organizational structure of the operational management can be designed using process approach. In project-oriented organizations and organisations with mixed-type activity (both operational and project), project management is performed by a special organizational structure (project office), or

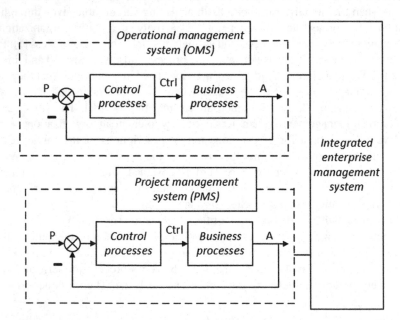

Fig. 1 Integrated enterprise management system structure (P—planned indicators; A—actual indicators; Ctrl—controlling actions). Objects of management are: the enterprise business processes and the project lifecycle processes. The enterprise management is performed within the organizational structure and controlled by regulations on the divisions functions and job descriptions of the employees

by a matrix structure combining operational and project management. To design such structures certain techniques are needed. When the enterprise management system is synthesized, it is necessary to create organizational structures sensibly, i.e. with reasonable number of employees, as well as job descriptions determining the functions and the amount of responsibility for each employee. It is, therefore, obvious, that a uniform methodological platform for synthesizing operational and project management systems is necessary.

The purpose of this paper is to demonstrate the advantages of the process approach as a uniform methodology for synthesizing an enterprise management system, and also the possibility to use this approach for designing a project management system.

2 Project Management Processes

When an operational management system, such as workflow management or planning and allocation of resources, is designed, the functioning of the management object (an enterprise or an organization) should be described in as many details as necessary. What is more, there are always a number of alternatives, which allows choosing the best variant in given conditions. It is advisable to describe business processes using one of the notations of structural modelling. The designed models should replicate the structure of the object functioning and the structure of the processes informational interactions, including management processes. Thus, structural models, as well as various choice models, allow for the analysis of variants and creation of optimized operational management systems. Basing on these systems, it is then possible to build information warehouses, electronic document management systems, and ERP systems. As a rule, this is the only approach that helps to make the expensive automation systems effective.

Let us now consider PMS according to the same parameters as operational management systems. PMS should have the goal and the object of management.

The project management objectives are usually set as follows [4, 5]:

- Project work scheduling and minimization deviations for dates of performance
- Calculating expenses and minimizing deviations from the set values
- Minimizing deviations from the set objectives and job quality

The objects of management are the project lifecycle processes.

The exact operational processes providing for the achievement of the specified objectives are, of course, not always the same. However, basing on the practical experience we can determine certain standard sets of such processes. As a model we have taken one of the most common standards—PMI standard, PMBOK guide [4].

According to it, project management processes can be divided in five groups: initiating process group, planning process group, execution process group, monitoring and controlling process group, and closing process group. Besides, the standard [4] provides classification of processes in the form of nine knowledge areas of project management. The general concept of operational processes of project management (management of a project lifecycle) is presented in Table 1 [4].

We shall consider these processes as objects for structural modelling. It is worth noticing that all of them are operational.

3   Project Management Process Modelling

Process modelling and analysis are the main components of the process approach. Structural models can demonstrate how the project management system functions. On their basis, it is possible to thoroughly analyse cause and effect relationships, estimate the workload, and perform an ABC analysis of the project lifecycle processes using simulation modelling.

Structural modelling also serves as a basis for various process automation systems. The processes given in Table 1 can be modelled using various notations, such as IDEF0, EPC, BPMN etc. The choice of notation usually depends on the required level of processes detalization. Thus, for a project oriented organization the highest detalization level can be reached through the interaction diagram of process groups (for one project) using IDEF0 notation (Fig. 2).

The IDEF0 diagram in Fig. 2 displaying groups of PMS processes, gives a general view of inputs and outputs of process groups determining their interaction, as well as tools for process management (arrows above) and execution mechanisms (arrows below). The process approach presupposes further decomposition of each group, which helps to see how the project management is performed (both generally and in details), and makes it possible to quickly adjust the composition and sequence of the processes, if necessary. Business process models are regulated by the following factors: the owners, the contractors, the execution duration and cost, and the planned KPI. Every operation process should have its owner and contractor. In organizational systems, they are the staff members grouped into certain organizational structures. Within the project, the owners and the contractors are appointed for operational processes from Table 1, which determines job descriptions and regulations on the activity of the PMS organizational structures. The model also allows (providing that the requests intensity is specified) to estimate the PMS labour intensity and the number of personnel needed.

The process execution algorithm is often described in details using EPC notation diagram (Fig. 3). EPC diagram shows the temporal sequence of process development stages influenced by functions (actions, operations, works). The diagram can also show the employees performing key functions, documents describing the process development, necessary tools, etc.

It is also necessary to analyse the logic consistency and ABC adequacy of the created models to the objectives. There is special software for model designing and analysing, such as ARIS, Business Studio etc. After the analysis, models can be corrected, if necessary. Based on such project management models, organizational structure, regulations on the divisions and job descriptions are then created.

Table 1 Project management processes classification according to PMBOK

Knowledge areas	Project management process groups				
	Initiating process group	Planning process group	Executing process group	Monitoring and controlling process group	Closing process group
Project integration management	Develop project Charter	Develop project management plan	Direct and manage project execution	Monitor and control project work; Perform integrated change control	Close project or phase
Project scope management		Collect requirements; Define scope; Create WBS		Verify scope; Control scope	
Project time management		Define activities; Sequence activities; Estimate activity resources; Estimate activity duration; Develop schedule		Control schedule	
Project cost management		Estimate cost; Determine budget		Control costs	
Project quality management		Plan quality	Perform quality assurance	Perform quality control	
Project HR management		Develop HR plan	Acquire project team; Develop project team; Manage project team		
Project communication management	Identify stakeholders	Plan communications	Distribute information; Manage stakeholder expectations	Report performance	
Project risk management		Plan risk management; Identify risks; Perform qualitative risk analysis; Perform quantitative risk analysis; Plan risk responses		Monitor and control risk	
Project procurement management		Plan procurements	Conduct procurements	Administer procurements	Close procurements

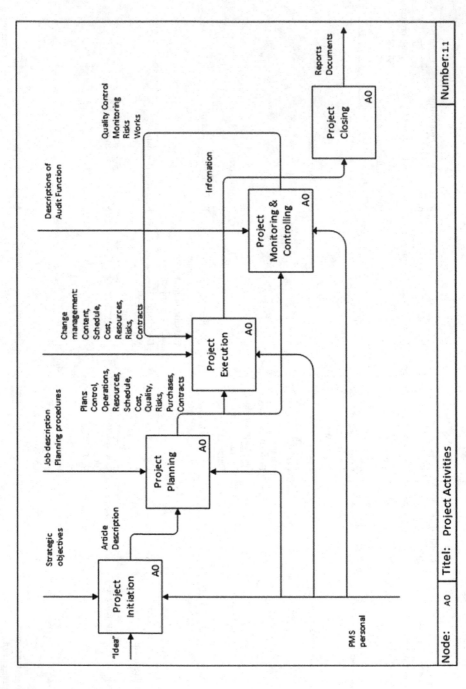

Fig. 2 An IDEF0 diagram of top level PMS processes

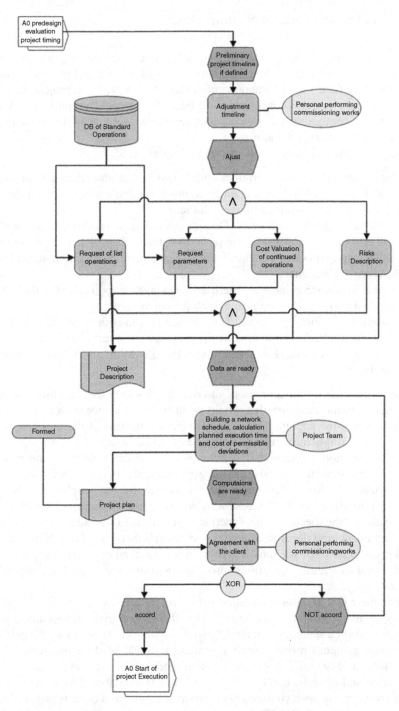

Fig. 3 A fragment of the EPC diagram of the process group "Planning"

4 Project Management System Design

There are various organizational management models determining allocation of
authority and responsibility. To this group belong functional and process models.
They both have their own advantages and disadvantages [1, 3]. In project management the process model is considered to be better for independent projects, and the
matrix model combining the process and functional approach—for mixed-type
activity—both operational and project.

The process model is based on several principles [1, 3]:

- Consolidation of several operations (functions) in one procedure performed by
  one subject (a contractor or a team of contractors). For example, functions 1–5
  and 7 in Fig. 3 are allocated to one contractor.
- Operational sequence continuity. Diverse operations carried out in a complete
  logical order are performed in one place by a team of specialists. For example,
  project planning processes on the diagram (Fig. 2) require operation managers as
  well as project designers.
- The process owner principle. There is a manager responsible for the whole
  project and coordination the results with the customer.
- The horizontal control principle. The consumer, who is the next element in the
  process chain, checks the quality of the previous stage result. For example, the
  planning process team (Fig. 2) estimates the quality of the initiating process
  performance.

One of the greatest advantages of the process model is that it allows creating
such organizational structure that would be in full compliance with the executed
processes due to the appointment of owners and contractors of the said processes,
which prevents duplication of responsibilities and irresponsibility zones.

The matrix model combines the principles of the functional and the process
systems. These structures consist of strongly regulated processes controlled by the
process manager. All the functions are performed by the employees who are
accountant for their operative functions to the process manager, but are still
subordinate to the head of the functional structure in an administrative way
[1]. When a structural division combines operational and project activity, the matrix
model can appear to be the most suitable. In this case, an employee may simultaneously conduct routine operational processes and manage project activity when
necessary.

When there is a great flow of requests for project activity and the workload for
the project management is as large as for the operational management, it as
advisable to form a separate structural division—a project office—that will perform
project management for one or several functional divisions of the enterprise.

In either case, organizational management models are based on the process and
works structural models. Each work (at the lower levels) and each process (at the
higher levels) has its own contractor or a group of contractors (a division), and each
process has its owner. Duration and cost of the process execution are estimated.
Process models determine the requirements to the project managers, their functions,

authority and responsibility. Thus, structural process models help to determine the staff list, the labour intensity and the cost of processes in project management.

Organizational and process structures together form a system of procedures and regulations describing interaction of separate contractors and divisions. The KPI determines the components of the project efficiency assessment. Together with the workflow structure, they provide for the electronic workflow system formation.

The suggested organizational model of project management can in turn, become a basis for forming requirements to project management automation system and its design.

5   Conclusion

The process approach serves as an effective methodology for constructing organizational management systems of an enterprise or an organization. Project management is an important component of organizational management. It seems to be reasonable to form organizational management system according to a uniform methodology—the process approach. The considered management processes of a project lifecycle (Table 1) are operational processes, which allows applying process approach to engineering PMS. For this purpose, it is necessary to formulate and specify the objectives and indicators of project management and to develop adequate to these objectives and indicators system of structural models of management processes for the project.

Structural models form a basis for synthesising organizational management, structure, regulations on the divisions and job descriptions, which together form the project organizational management model. However, there are no well-known examples of project management systems implementation.

For many enterprises and organizations combining operational and project activity, the availability of the formalized methods of project management system engineering is necessary. The suggested method seems to be of certain value considering the fact that it allows to develop integrated operational and project management system based on the same methodology.

References

1. Pinaev, D. A. (2012). Process management - What is best? *BOSS, 3*.
2. Project Management. (2012). *Requirements for project management* (12 p.). GOST R 54869—2011. Moscow: Standartinform.
3. Becker, J., Vilkov, L., Taratoukhine, V., Kugeler, M., & Rosemann, M. (Eds.). (2010). *Process management (Менеджмент процессов)*. Moscow: Eksmo.
4. PMBOK Guide. (2008). *PMBOK Guide 4th Edition (руководство PMBOK)* (241 pp.). Project Management Institute, Inc.
5. Trotsky, M., Grucha, B., & Ogonyok, K. (2006). *Project management*. Moscow: Finance and Statistics. 304 pp.

Towards to Enhancing Business Process Management in Corporate Environment: Emerging Markets View

Anastasia Pozdnyakova, Victoria Sheer, Yury Kupriyanov, Victor Taratukhin, and Joerg Becker

Abstract Social BPM (BPM) is widely discussed in the scientific and business community. While the interest to the topic is elevating, the potential and benefits of employing Social BPM remain vague and ambiguous. This paper discusses these problems and elaborates on two different approaches of Social BPM: external and internal. Internal approach is about designing and modeling business processes inside the organization by all employees, who are insiders to the processes, while external is about participating and listening to all stakeholders such, as employees, current customers, potential customers, competitors and suppliers. We examined emerging markets, particularly Russia, to evaluate the spread of Social BPM there. The practice of integrating such tools in National Research University Higher School of Economics (Moscow, Russia) is presented and the research was conducted to estimate stakeholders' attitude to the system.

Keywords Social BPM • BPM • Social software • Social media • Knowledge management

1 Introduction

The problem of value for commercial and public organizations is becoming more and more popular within academia and business environment. Numerous conferences and conferences' tracks are organized to discuss this topic. For example, Sandy Kemsley presented her work "Making Social BPM Mean Business" at the conference BPM 2012, where she talked about benefits, which social BPM can bring to business. Emanuele Molteni and Marco Brambilla hold a talk on "Social BPM", (BPM Europe 2012, London, June, 19), where they disguised the influence of Social Web and BPM combination on performance of an organization. Social

A. Pozdnyakova • V. Sheer • Y. Kupriyanov (✉)
National Research University Higher School of Economics, Moscow, Russia
e-mail: yury.kupriyanov@sap.com

V. Taratukhin • J. Becker
European Research Center for Information Systems, WWU Muenster, Münster, Germany

© Springer International Publishing Switzerland 2016   31
J. Becker et al. (eds.), *Emerging Trends in Information Systems*, Progress in IS,
DOI 10.1007/978-3-319-23929-3_4

Business Forum, which took place at Milan, 4–5 June, 2012 was totally devoted to this problem [1].

Management world have already known that the company's main resource is knowledge, since 1993 Peter Drucker in his book "Post-Capitalist Society" said, that the World comes into "knowledge society" where the main recourse is not capital, natural recourses or labor, and the main role in the company is performed by "knowledge workers" or knowledge employees [2].

It is a well-known fact that Web 2.0 helps companies to develop, evolve and to use this "knowledge" in a better way (McKinsey Global Survey, September 2009; [3]) [4]. The question that we want to investigate is how BPM can benefit from social software as one of the Web 2.0 instances. It should be mentioned, that a company, which can use Social BPM features usually represents innovative, fast developing market with non-standardized goods. It means that it is hard for such companies to "stay afloat" and it is "remaining in the dark", so almost all its processes are hard to define.

The purpose of this paper is to represent two different approaches of applying Web 2.0 to improve BPM at the company, what is known as Social BPM, and to examine specificity of its usage on the emerging markets (especially Russia). The tasks, which were set, are the following:

- Define and describe two approaches to Social BPM exploitation
- Highlight their weak and strong points
- Investigate the problem of Social BPM spread and use in Russia

The paper is organized into two parts. The first part consists of four sections:

- Section 1 gives definitions of considered aspects.
- Sections 2 and 3 describe two different approaches to the problem.
- Section 4 presents comparison of the approaches.

The second part represents an overview of the spread of Social BPM tools in Russia. Also, it was attempted to make some recommendations concerning the improvement of the Social BPM dissemination in emerging markets. Finally, the paper ends with conclusion, reflection and discussion of the further research.

2 Existing Approaches Analysis

2.1 BPM Meets Social Software

Business Process Management is a set of structured methods and technologies for managing the operations of an organization [5]. "The goal of BPM is to create a process-centric, customer-focused organization that integrates management, people, process and technology for both operational and strategic improvement"

[6]. Classically, the focus of BPM has been transactional, highly repetitive processes that can be predicted and executed according to a schema [7].

It is known, that this attitude supposes a top-down approach. Today, however, bottom-up and especially center-up-down approaches [8] are becoming more popular and communication among people can improve their applying and can help to exclude problems, which were identified above.

It is obvious that communication is inseparable from social software. Social software has been defined by Schmidt and Nurcan [3] as "software that supports the interaction of human beings and production of artifacts by combining the input from independent contributors without predetermining the way to do this". It can be asserted that social technology can support a more flexible, human-centric approach to BPM. That is what Social BPM is about. The movement to Social BPM is evidenced in the literature by Silva [9] who discusses the view that business processes should not hinder human intervention, and the social technology should be embedded within BPM initiatives.

Social business process management is an emerging concept that marries the flexibility and pervasiveness of social media with the management discipline of BPM [10]. Marco Brambilla from Politecnico di Milano (Italy), in turn, defines Social BPM as "the effort of designing and executing business processes collaboratively". On the basis of these two definitions, it can be said that social BPM can help companies to:

• Involve their informal knowledge to the working process
• Make all processes in the company more visible to the affected stakeholders
• Raise the awareness of the community about this processes
• Find appropriate performers for processes execution
• Elicit opinions that can contribute to make a right decision

The theme of social BPM is under discussion and there is no comprehension, what it is exactly, however academia and business communities have already understood the importance and efficiency of social BPM. Different experts see the realization of this concept in various ways. Some experts believe that a company should develop its own application (or to buy it) which connects Enterprise Social Network and BPM. Others suggest using already existing global social services and incorporating them into company's business processes. Two approaches were identified based on these opinions. The first approach will be called internal, because it includes only internal stakeholders of a company and support business process management itself. The second will be named external as it engages users of global social networks and serves as a mean for future development and improvement of the business processes and models.

2.2 Social BPM as Corporate Application

There are different issues connected with BPM and Social Software. During BPMS2 workshop some BPM phenomena were identified. They show the importance of adding Web 2.0 techniques to BPM.

1. Model-Reality Divide. This is the divide between abstract process models and the executed processes. It means that, in spite of the fact that business process models can be well designed, they are not used during the enactment of business process. Unsurprisingly, the employees do not accept such models but follow their own process. They just don't want to go deep into the model and continue repeating the process to which they are accustomed to.
2. Lost innovation. Although there is knowledge in the organization about possible improvements of business processes, this knowledge is not applied and the possible optimizations are omitted. It happens because such knowledge does not reach the process owner.
3. Information pass-on threshold. The previous problem appears because it needs too much effort to the author of the improvement to pass it to the owner of the process. Further, processing is not transparent to employees or success is considered to be improbable.
4. Lack of information fusion. It means that stakeholders are not properly involved into business processes modeling; consequently they are only "consumers", who have to accept processes created for them. Moreover, the terms and concepts just imposed on the employees [9].

Thereby, combining social tools with BPM is necessary for improving organization's business processes and for making them more applicable. Different researches stick to this idea. They believe that social software can support involving employees, customers and other stakeholders in the BPM lifecycle. Professors from Queensland University of Technology consider that social technology can be applied to each phase of BPM process lifecycle [7]. They compared BPM phases of BPM lifecycle, which were assigned by Prof. Becker, Prof. Kugeler & Prof. Roseman in 2001 [11] to the framework of the list of characteristics that define what social technology can offer [12]. It is presented in the table below. This Table 1 shows how Web 2.0 concepts could be used for BPM lifecycle.

This comparison leads us to the understanding of importance of social technology for BPM. The question, which rises, is how to connect Web 2.0 with business processes of the company.

Social features can be introduced at multiple levels while designing BPM solutions. An evolutionary perspective on social BPM adoption model is presented on Fig. 1.

At the first (lower) level there are the conventional BPM solutions, which are implemented today very often. The main characteristic of this solution is a rigid task and no communication between process participants. The next step is collaborative process design, which allows people to design business processes

Table 1 BPM lifecycle and Web 2.0 patterns (Paul Mathiasen [7])

Lifecycle phase	Phase description	O'Reilly's core patterns for Web 2.0 success							
		Collective intelligence	"Intel inside"	Innovation	User experience	Pervasive software	Perpetual beta	Long tail	Scalable
Process identification	Understand the process scope and eco-system in detail	X	X					X	
Process modeling	Represent the identified process via modeling language	X							
Process analysis	Analyze process performance and issues	X	X	X					
Process improvement (to-be)	Identify and evaluate options for process improvement, consider constraints/resources	X	X	X	X	X	X	X	X
Process implementation	Embed improved process in the Organization			X	X	X	X	X	X
Process execution (to-do)	Perform the processes manually or automatically			X	X		X	X	X
Process monitoring and control	Guiding and controlling the daily operations		X			X	X	X	

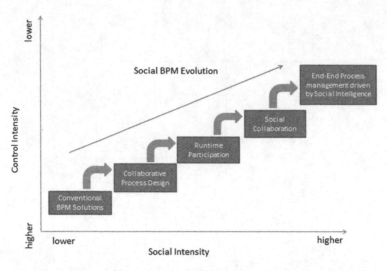

Fig. 1 An evolutionary perspective on social BPM adoption (Infosys Research, 2011)

collectively. It provides many benefits if the BPM team are geographically dispersed. After that comes runtime participation, which can help to extend collaboration from process design to process execution. It can be realized through the social tools, such as chat voting mechanisms etc., which are integrated into the BPM system environment. Next, there is a social collaboration, which involves participants in the process execution by the social media, who were not envisaged to be a part of that process during deployed time. At the last stage end to end processes are designed and managed by social intelligence, which includes the "feedback loop". After the consideration of this evolutionary perspectives of Social BPM it can be said that tandem of social tools and BPM has great opportunities for future progress. To achieve these levels of evolution, different approaches of business processes development are used. Below are introduced some methods of combining BPM with Web 2.0 techniques.

Model-Driven Method

The method for the design, fast prototyping and deployment of BPM solutions extended with social collaborations, which refer to the fourth stage of this evolution, was introduced by professors of Politecnico di Milano at their paper "A Model-driven approach to Social BPM applications" [13]. The core of the proposed approach is three-layered:

1. Methodological level. It provides a structure for deep understanding of the incorporate social interactions ways in business processes.

2. Notational level. Here they verify the capacity of a BPMN language in order to express social communications and cover Social BPM requirements (they call it BPMN 2.0).
3. Technical level. At this level they exploit model-driven software engineering techniques to produce applications. This technique helps to bring social process directly from the extended BPMN process schema.

This approach can be prototyping by the use of WebRatio service (it represents the model-driven software engineering technique, that was mentioned), which helps to build different innovative application, such as user-centric BPM systems and Social BPM. The team of WebRatio company declares that they are "focusing on the most challenging aspect of Social BPM: letting organization harness the power of the crowd by allowing selected and controlled social interactions within business process". WebRatio allows its customers to transform project idea into the functioning solution in three steps. Firstly, a model in BPMN and WebML has to be designed. Secondly, an environment needs to be customized. Finally, WebRatio is able to generate the web-based application. Moreover, this service can be used in many other cases, which refer to the Social BPM development.

Recommendational-Based Method

The other method for enhancing BPM with social features was suggested by Agnes Koschmider in her work "Social Software for Modeling Business Processes". It expresses a recommendation-based process modeling support system which is supplemented by the "social" features. In her work social networks from a process model repository and from a recommendation history are proposed. Through such social extension process builders "can gain insight into already selected and reused specific process models". As it can be seen such system refers to the last stage of the Social BPM evolution.

Such recommendation system can suggest process fragments to modelers by the use of their modeling intention as hatched from the user's interest. In order to use this system in practice developers offer a query interface and an automatic recommender component, which can predict necessary process model fragments. Of course, such application is suitable for standard processes with standard parts.

Agnes Koschmider in her paper [14] identified some benefits, which such system elaborates:

- Strategic colaboration support
- User trust behavior and mutual support encouragement (e.g. people can see in table-based results list which person belong to recommended process fragment, it meant that people can consult the social network if they have some doubt)
- Process changes propagation

Moreover, this recommendation system allows users to estimate the degree of fitness of a b-p model part, which was recommended. In can be proposed, that the prototype of recommendation system, which was described in Koschmider [14] relates to a sphere of society where process modeling is seen as "an act that is better performed collaboratively". It supports an enabling practice of extending a repository by building-in a feature of adding high-quality models with custom elements developed by users.

Shared Spaces Method

The method, based on the concept of shared spaces was introduced in the article "In Search of the Holy Grail: Integrating social software with BPM Experience report" by Ilia Bider. He described two systems, which realize this concept, and the latest system is based on the previous one. These systems refer to third stage of Social BPM evolution. Authors believe that shared space solves a problem with a decision about how much information needed to be sent to a person to allow him to complete the task. Therefore, in these systems there is no information flow, it means that a person is invited to visit a shared space and complete a task in it with the supposition that all necessary information is already there. The first application, called ProBis, allows users, which were invited by the other user, to join to the process's modeling and execution and to make changes in its model and in other documents, connected to the process. Also, it is possible to communicate with other participants of the process. The good thing about this system is that in saves the historical information about the process instance, and in future it can be used to model and execute similar processes.

iPB, the second application, is a tool for developing systems like ProBis, but with the following changes. In this system a shared space is divided into subspaces, which are placed in the recommended direction of movement. When a participant joins the shared space, he can click on the box, which embodies the part of the process, and find there necessary information.

Both these systems show the same method of integrating social techniques into BPM. The first application has a rich functionality, but has some problems with visualization of structured processes. Moreover, it requires training before employees would be capable of using it in practice. The second system, on the contrary, has highly visual interface, which is easy to understand, but today it lacks some functionality, which is available in the first system [15].

Resume

The methods, which were described above can be assumed as the basis of the corporate application for integrating social tools into BPM. It is of primary importance for every organization to develop its own system or changes and adapt the existing one due to the fact that organization has its own set of business processes; moreover the same business process in different organizations can be executed differently and can consist of different steps.

Business processes in commercial organizations can be enhanced by social tools. But is the developing of a corporate application for integrating social features into BPM the only way to improve it? The corporate system unites only the employees of the company, but some business processes can be enhanced by external stakeholders much more effectively than by internal. Some business process can be also improved by taking into account opinion of current and future consumers of the company's products. In the next chapter the methods of such improving and some examples will be illustrated.

2.3 Social media and BPM

The growth of social media over the last 5 years has been spectacular. Demographically the users of social networks tend to be a younger generation—especially 17–30 age groups. As of July 2011, there were officially more than 750 million active users of Facebook alone (Statistics from the web-site socialnomics.net). Twitter and LinkedIn also have millions of active users. Therefore, the current young generation is growing up getting accustomed to communicate with each other via Social Networks. The business world, not to be left behind, is rapidly adopting social media platforms for various reasons, which range from having a social media presence aligned with the business strategy, end-consumer engagement, creating and enhancing the brand image and as an additional lever for revenue generation. It is explainable because today, 93 % of online consumers expect companies to have a social media presence [16].

External approach can improve BPM of the company through different methods. In the first method data from social networks such as Facebook, Twitter, LinkedIn, Foursquare, Google + will be analyzed. The other method is about developing social BPM community. The last method is about developing an Enterprise social network (ESN).

Social Networks

The purposes of using the first method can be different. Employees of particular departments can scan data from public social media, customer conversations about a product, and use this information to improve quality of their goods. For organizations such platforms enable to create a communication channel to their customers and to observe, listen and respond to the customer's feedback in real time. Roughly speaking, the customer can be engaged in the life of the company through three phases, which are shown on Fig. 2.

Customer Acquisition is the process of acquiring new customers. Customer Servicing is the process of addressing the customer's requirements. Customer Relationship Management is the process of handling any changes according to the customer's request.

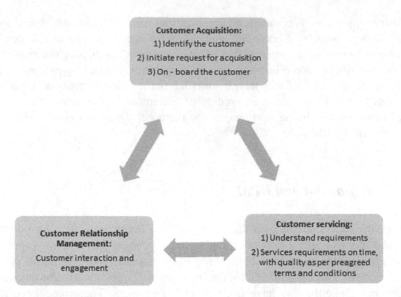

Fig. 2 The three phases of customer engagement [16]

The other processes, which can be enhanced by social media tools:

1. HR. The LinkedIn can enrich this process, because it contains millions of CV of different potential applicants. Also some recruiters also scan through the accounts at social networks of people, which they want to hire, to see some personal information, hobbies, and statuses. IT companies can also recruit people, who are strongly involved in IT forum, have their own opinion. Four of five companies today use social media in their HR processes [17].
2. Marketing. In social media web-sites it is possible to find the opinion of customers about your products. Nearly one third of bloggers regularly post their opinion about trademarks and brands [17]. Also company can add videos, mini-surveys, photos, some themes for discussion about their products and then explore the comments. For this purpose the best sites are: Facebook, different blogs and forums.
3. R&D. Some opinions of the customers can define the directions of future researches. The popularity of YouTube and the use of videos from these web-sites at social networks forced companies to download their commercial and instructional videos there. Also companies can read comments, which are left by consumers below these videos.

These processes are only examples of how operational processes can be enhanced by social networks. Any company can use it for any process it wants.

Using this approach, companies can capture feedback by creating new vectors for input. There are some examples of applying it.

- One financial institution changed its debit card policy. This policy was about denying the transaction instead of charging an overdraft fee. They looked through the social media web-sites and saw that their customers did not like it. The bank responded by changing its policy [18] ·
- One electronic company that produces accessories looked through the opinions of early iPad owners on social media, which were about their iPad. This company let these opinions drive their product strategy and it brought very strong results. .
- KLM Royal Dutch Airlines identified their frequent Flyers by scanning the people, who use Twitter at the airport. To thank them for their loyalty KLM surprised them with the small present, which was based on their preferences, which were defined by their account at social media web-sites [10]
- One bank wanted to launch a new credit card, targeted at college students. To segment target audience it looked through students' accounts at Twitter. Then it examined their twits and sent adds to students, who might be interested in it. After that students' responses were analyzed [16]

Social BPM Community

Social BPM community can be intended to be a vendor-neutral place, where people doing processes discovery will share ideas and collaborate on process discovery. There some documents, articles and there authors will be found. So business architects of a company will not be alone with their processes, trying to find some practice and books. In this community everybody will be able to find process they need and to talk to its developer.

There are already some examples of such communities:

1. The Aris business process modeling software online community, which has more than 100,000 subscribers, among which are heads of business architecture and repository management.
2. Accenture has the community of such type, BPM Champions, but it is internal. This portal contains links to process best practices and articles. There are tools for contacting other members of the community like blogs [10].

Using this method can improve all business processes of the company, because there information about any of them can be found.

Enterprise Social Network

This network can span both the employees and the clients; it has features like blogs, wikis, chat-tools. ESN can also unite all companies of the same industry or type globally or from one country [19]. This network provides the company a direct channel to connect with its customers. They can be quickly informed about new products; also their requirements and complaints will be quickly analyzed and responded. It increases customer-centricity. The ESN platform for companies of the same industry can help them to get together and finalize the liability split, which can save a lot of back and forth communications between them and significantly enhance customer experience. The example of the realization of such method can be seen at the White paper by Infosys, 2012.

The use of ESN, which spans companies with their clients, can improve business processes, which are closely connected with the clients, such as sales, marketing, servicing and so on. The use of the ESN of the second type can enhance all business processes. This happens because companies of the same industry are able to exchange there their experiences of modeling and executing their business processes; and, of course, some of them can be similar to b-p of the company of the same industry.

Today to stay competitive company has to evolve fast; use contemporary hardware, software, SaaS; be well informed about constantly changing customers' preferences. The fastest and the cheapest way to do so is the using of Social Media, which provides enormous quantity of information. This information must be analyzed, for example using social mining techniques, and applied in the alteration of company's business processes. The methods of applying it range from business processes reengineering to only adding such boxes as "Twit about new product" in the model of the b-p. These measures will help company to stay competitive and increase customers' loyalty. The point above told about which Social networks can be used to do this.

Approaches Comparison (Who Is the Winer?)

In previous sections two different approaches were examined. The question, that rises, which approach the company should apply? To understand it, the weak and strong sides of the two considered approaches have to be identified. The comparison will be made through using the following criteria:

• Processes
• Trust
• Ease of use
• Ease of involvement
• Control

The first criterion provides information about processes which can be improved by using external or internal approach to Social BPM. The greatest benefit of introducing Social BPM gains the companies or departments, which produce non-standardized goods and services and opinion of the customers is very important for them, the best opportunities to take customers' opinion into account provides external approach. There are also benefits of using Social BPM when the modeling and executing of the process demand a high level of communication and collaboration among the performing actors, especially when two or more subdivisions are

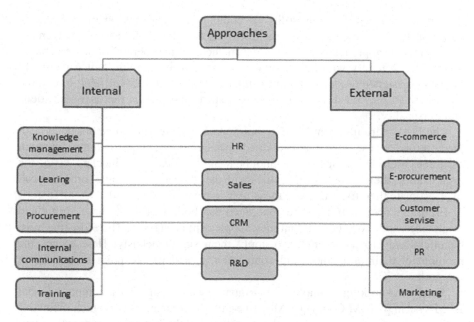

Fig. 3 Employment of social BPM approaches to business processes

involved, there the most effective will be internal approach. Figure 3 shows information about processes, which can be enhanced by Social BPM.

Trust is very important criterion. It represents the degree of trust between people, which are involved in the Social BMP employment. Heider's "balance theory" [20] suggests that individuals are likely to interact with fiends or with people, about whom they heard than with unknown people. Moreover, 80 % of people trust opinion of their on-line friends more than their real ones [17]. Hence, in the company the same tendency can appear. This is more about internal approach: users may be willing to trust and follow the advices of proved persons. In the external approach this problem is different: employees understand that the users are unlikely to provide them with accurate information, but they also know that if this information is well analyzed it can be very useful.

Ease of use criterion reflects the amount of time and qualification which would require employees to learn to work with the tool. While social media tools are easy to use for all types of users, social software tools require special knowledge and deep understanding of the b-p models. To make the understanding easier the internal systems have to be well visualized, company has to organize some training, the interface must be intuitively clear. However, the use of external approach raises the problem of finding the appropriate information.

Talking about the ease of involvement it is necessary to stress, that in the external social tools (especially in the communities) it is difficult to involve stakeholders, because they are accustomed to work in one way and they do not want to change anything. Moreover, they may not understand for what needs do they have to use it, but the utility of communities depends on the amount of participants and if there are a few members it is not effective. Ease of involvement in the internal approach depends on the method. In the method of shared spaces there is no difficulty with the involvement, because people are invited there and they have assigned tasks. For recommendation systems it is not difficult too. In the model-driven method difficulties of involvement depends on the user's positions and personality.

The last criterion is control. External approach represents some obstacles with the control, because it have dynamic and open environment. Also, in this approach malicious users and competitors cannot be identified clearly and blocked. Inside the organization, there are a few difficulties with the control, for example some user can over-estimate their expertise and these users have to be identified.

From this comparison can be concluded that both approaches have strong and weak sides, and it can be said that they supplement each other. Therefore, the most beneficial way to use them is to apply them simultaneously. Here comes the problem of their integration and connection, it will be the point of our future research.

Today, the striking example of a company, which can offer a complete Social BPM system, is IBM Company. Moreover, they offer application which maintains not only the one approach (external or internal), but the two approaches at the same time. This application is known as Blueworks Live [21]. It is needed to be said that the most meaningful functions of this SaaS service are collaborative process discovery/analysis, business-processes template library, features of the knowledge community (blogs, forums), high-level process modeling, extended social team-work and rapid, lightweight process automation (by creating 'Process Apps', in which people can carry out activities, add attachments and comment to the instance they are working on, and they can redirect work to other users). IBM team said, that the main purpose of the Blueworks Live is "to focus on helping tackle the many dozens or hundreds of lightweight processes that are not properly supported with IT today" [21]. As it can be seen all these features belong to internal approach. But this servise also creates the availability of public streams. It means that social collaboration within internal stakeholders is available. For example, IBM uses relevant Twitter updated from individuals and companies, which can have important BPM expertise.

Of course, the IBM product is one of the most functional Social BPM System today, but even this service do not involve all existing features of external and internal approaches. It is clear, that today the field of Social BPM is developing fast all over the World, and there is a hope, that soon we will have a real Social BPM systems market. There are some countries, however, in which the theme of Social BPM began to appear among academia and especially business sphere quite recently. In the next part of this paper, the Social BPM situation in one of such countries will be examined.

3 Social BPM in Russia

Countries of emerging markets, such as BRIC countries: Brazil, Russia, India, China and South Africa have great prospects and opportunities for IT development and diffusion. However, new technologies adopt there more slowly, than in the USA or Europe [22]. In this paper the Russian situation in the Social BPM is analyzing.

Today in Russia the point of Social BPM has just appeared, consequently, information about this theme is almost unavailable. So as in the World there are even no complete Social BPM systems (instead of IBM Blueworks Live), in Russia it is no full understanding, what Social BPM and systems, based on this concept are.

Concerning this topic, it can be said that in Russia there are only concepts and ideas, but not the working applications. However, some aspects of social software can be found in different applications, which are used in companies. For example, there is a system known as "Comindware", which was developed by Russian scientists Maksim Chiplyaev and Petr Volynskiy in 2010, but it is sold out mostly in USA and Europe [23]. This system represents Social BPM application type (as IBM BlueWorks live, but its function is much poorer). It has some social features, which this application supports: comments, file stream, tasks management. In spite of the fact, that it is Russian product, in our country only a few people know about it. Another application from Russian developers is Alvex system. This product can be named as a type of Social BPM, because it is a BPM system (or even ECM/BPM) which provides an opportunity to develop ESN and it also supports Google Docs [24]. The system, which resembles Social BPM application was suggested and realized by the Russian company "IT" and HSE Center of Technologies of Information Management [25]. This system looks for experts in different fields inside the company and its decisions are based on mining e-mails and search requests of the employees.

There is no doubt, that in some Russian companies (frequently in IT companies) there are "hand-made" social applications, which can be build-in in different ERP, BPM, CRM systems, or which simply represent enterprise communities. Many international companies which have their branch in Russia also use applications, which involve social software and media features, for example SAP Company and its department University Alliances have their own communities, which allow employees and other stakeholders to communicate and solve their problems in this corporate social network. However such information is private. In Russia the best way to find out about such information is to participate in different BPM conferences.

Nevertheless we can give information about our own experience connected with Social BPM. We represent the Higher School of Economics, and it has its own social network, which can be considered as an example of internal approach. This social network is known as "HSE Educational Information Environment" or how students call it LMS. It has access to: the information about courses and timetables, required materials. There are tools to send email or have a chat with students and

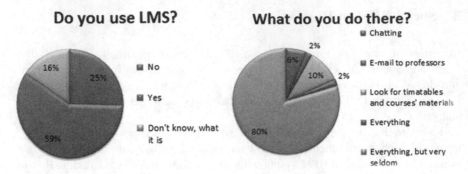

Do you use LMS?

- No
- Yes
- Don't know, what it is

16%
25%
59%

What do you do there?

- Chatting
- E-mail to professors
- Look for timatables and courses' materials
- Everything
- Everything, but very seldom

2%
6%
10%   2%
80%

Fig. 4 Student LMS usage habits

professors. In addition, soon it would be possible to view your mark-book, to create group projects and comment all related activities, to pass different tests. For professors it would be possible to export the students' marks to Excel and analyze them. The office of the head of studies can easily interact with all students and lecturers using LMS. According to this information it can be said that many business-processes of HSE take place in this network. In spite of this range of possible activities this network is not popular among students, which was concluded from the represented below research, so they use for the same purposes other sources. It leads to the declining utility of this network as the application for the realization HSE's business-processes.

The research was conducted to find out students' attitude to LMS. The charts below represent its results. The charts at Fig. 4 reflect that developing a functional system is not enough; this system has to be convenient and widely-advertised. Stakeholders have to understand for what reasons they need this system, otherwise it won't work because the fewer people use such systems, the less effective it is.

The situation, concerning external approach is similar to the represented above. Social media is widespread in Russia. General situation in Russian social media market is the following [26]:

- The growth of social networks users has slowed down (from 19.4 % in 2010 to 11.2 in 2012)
- More than one third of social networks users in the Eastern Europe are Russian people.
- Total amount of social networks users in Russia is 51, eight million in 2012.
- Most often, old and middle-age people do not use social networks and services; they can only serve the Internet some times.

Russian companies use social media much more frequently if they sell or distribute products or services and their target audience are at the age of 15–30 years. There are also many companies, which help to advertise products through social media. Ninety percent of business-processes of such companies are at social media. The same HSE uses Vkontakte to improve its business-processes and connect with stakeholders. It has several communities in this social network, where administrators can post some news, surveys, announcements and students are able to discuss it there. Using these communities, HSE collects information in which it is interested in and makes some resumes. Social services as Facebook, Twitter or LinkedIn are widely used in our country, but we have our own social networks which are much more widespread in Russia. For example, social networks known as Vkontakte and Odnoklassniki. They are very similar to Facebook, and these services have different audience. Service Vkontakte usually is used by younger people, and Odnoklassniki, in contrary, preferred by the oldest ones. At Vkontakte there are different communities of interests, where people discuss the current situation in their field. There are many IT communities, which have as its members both IT specialists and representatives of other fields. Such communities can be used as Social BPM communities. Also many companies have their communities at Vkontakte, where they advertise their products, discuss new feature and customers' wants, respond to customers' complains and requests. Social media is also used in Russia in HR. Many companies look through candidate's accounts at social networks before hiring him. Russian experts from the "Logika Biznesa 2.0" company suggest that Social BPM in Russia can be widely used in the freelancing market. This can be made by using, for example, crowdsourcing platform Openidea.pro.

Some managers of Russia companies, however, do not support the idea of integration social media into business processes. For example, General Manager of the company ELMA Andrey Budin supposes that internal commercial information cannot be mixed up with public information in the network [1].

It can concluded, that the use of social media in business sphere is rather widespread, but only a few people think about Social BPM as the tool for improving business-processes. Russian expert in this sphere Andrey Koptelov believes that Social BPM will become widespread only when economic crisis leads to the overabundance of labor force and therefore employees become more initiative (Cnews, 2012).

The analysis that was held in the second part brought us hope, that the first complete Russian Social BPM system do not make us wait and that business community will soon realize how many benefits can Social BPM bring them. It is very important to create a right communication scheme between business and academia in Russia to reach an appropriate degree of the Social BPM development.

4 Conclusion

Combining social software and media tools with business processes management allows company to receive a number of benefits by integration employees into BPM. The opportunity to involve all employees breaks the barrier of knowledge creation and diffusion. Social features have the potential to increase not only knowledge but collaborative intensive business processes; it can speed up decision making and improve the global reactivity of the company. To get this opportunity company has to create the right corporate environment and trust culture, otherwise, social tools will not work.

BPM and social tools in tandem offer new possibilities for the business processes designing. In the company it has to be considered how b-p design can be realized and supported with the instruments provided by social tools. Different approaches of this realization have been discussed in this paper.

It was established that Social BPM can be effectively used internally to share information, knowledge, solutions within a company and externally facilitating new processes, their changes and reaching out external stakeholders. Moreover, it was recommended to use Social BMP in these two ways simultaneously to reach all possible benefits.

In this paper a view was expressed that Social BPM in all countries, especially in Russia, is a very nascent area and it has not been adopted widespread yet. Despite this World situation, some companies have already offered complete Social BPM systems. At the same time, in Russia some steps toward social tools in BPM were made and different discussions about this tandem on the BPM forums were conducted.

The goal of the future research will be concentrated on the analysis of the Social BPM practices. For this purpose the data warehouse will be created and information about companies' revenues and other KPIs after Social BPM implementation will be collected and analyzed in this DW using data mining techniques. However, to conduct this research some time has to pass until sufficient quantity of companies implement Social BPM tools.

Social BPM is a great and powerful concept for process-driven companies, where there no established in an explicit and concise manner processes. It can help such organizations to stay competitive and to become adaptive to changes.

References

1. BPM for Business. (2012). http://www.cnews.ru/reviews/index.shtml?2012/10/05/505579_1. Retrieved on October 28, 2012.
2. Drucker, P. (1993). *Post-capitalist society*. New York: Harper Business.
3. Schmidt, R., & Nurcan, S. (2009). BPM and social software. *Business Process Management Workshops, 17*, 649–658.
4. Sandy, K. (2010). *Enterprise 2.0 meets business process management international handbooks on information systems 2010* (pp. 565–574). Berlin: Springer.
5. ABPMP. (2009). *Guide to the business process management common bony of knowledge (BPM COK)* 2 ed.
6. Goeke, R. J., & Antonucci, Y. L. (2011). Antecedents to job success in BPM: A comparison of two models. *Information Resources Management Journal, 24*(1), 46–65.
7. Mathiasen, P. (2011). Applying social technology to business process lifecycle management. In *The 4th workshop on business process management and social software*.
8. Nonaka, I., & Takeuchi, H. (1995). *The knowledge-creating company: How Japanese companies create the dynamics of innovation*. New York: Oxford University Press.

9. Erol, S. (2010). Combining BPM and social software: Contradiction of chance? *Journal of Software Maintenance and Evolution: Research and Practice, 22*(6–7), 449–476.
10. Franz, P., & Kirchmer, M. (2012). *Social BPM. Engaging people in value-driven BPM*. http://www.accenture.com/SiteCollectionDocuments/PDF/Accenture-Social-BPM-Engaging-People-in-Value-driven-BPM.pdf. Retrieved on November 27, 2012.
11. Becker, J., Kugeler, M., & Rosemann, M. (2001). *Business process lifecycle management*. White paper.
12. O'Reilly, T., & Musser, J. (2006). *Web 2.0 principles and best practices*. O'Reilly Radar.
13. Brambilla, M. (2012). Combining social web and BPM for improving enterprise performances: The BPM4People approach to Social BPM. In *Proceeds of the world wide web conference* (pp. 223–226).
14. Koschmider, A. (2010). Social software for modeling business processes. *Journal of Information Technology, 25*(3), 308–315, 322.
15. Bider, I. (2010). In search of the holy grail: Integrating social software with BPM. Experience report. In *BPMSD 2010 proceedings*.
16. Murphy, N., & Whelan, S. (2012). *Social media and business processes management (BPM) enable customer-centricity*. http://www.wipro.com/Documents/Social%20MediaBPM-Whitepaper.pdf. Retrieved on October 04, 2012.
17. 40 Facts About Social Networks. (2012). http://www.adme.ru/research/40-faktov-o-socialnyh-setyah-433005/. Retrieved on October 28, 2012.
18. Olding, E., & Rozewll, J. (2010). *Social BPM: Design by doing*. Gartner.
19. Krishnamurthy, S. (2012). *Social process design, execution and intelligence for a better customer experience*. http://www.infosys.com/BPM-EAI/resource-center/Documents/social-design-execution-intelligence.pdf. Retrieved on October 10, 2012.
20. Heider, F. (1996). *The psychology of interpersonal relations*. Chichester: Wiley.
21. Ward-Dutton, N. (2010). *Vendor insight. IBM breaks new ground with Blueworks live*. Premium Advisory Report MWD Advisors.
22. Taratoukhin, V. (2012). How ICT influence on BPM in small and medium-sized enterprises of emerging markets. *Business-Informatics Journal, 3*.
23. Comindware - Free Intranet System for Task Management. (2012). http://www.intranetno.ru/tags/COMINDWARE/. Retrieved on October 12, 2012.
24. Alvex - Russian software on the basis of Alfresco. (2012). http://www.intranetno.ru/tags/ALVEX/. Retrieved on October 12, 2012.
25. "IT" Company and HSE Center of Technologies of Information Management Have Developed the Freelancing-Search System. (2012). http://www.ural.it.ru/press_center/news/AyTi_i_NIU_VSHE_razrabotali_korporativnuu_sistemu_poiska_ekspertov_. Retrieved on October 05, 2012.
26. Growth of the Russian Social Networks Users. (2012). http://cossa.ru/news/247/25616/. Retrieved on October 14, 2012.

Business Architecture Development and Process and Project Maturity

Igor V. Ilin, Anastasia I. Lyovina, and Anton R. Antipin

Abstract **Purpose** Business architecture is the basis for the development and implementation of information systems. In turn the basis for business architecture are business processes and project portfolio. The article is aimed at the development of theoretical foundation of business architecture design on the basis of such business technologies as business process management and the corporate standard of project management.

Design/methodology/approach The article analyses the place and role of business processes and projects within the enterprise architecture as well as the interdependence between maturity levels of process and project management in order to develop the approach to the design of the balanced business architecture of a process and project oriented company.

Findings Maturity of project management depends on the maturity of process management. In turn, the maturity of process management is determined by the capabilities of the company to implement projects for the re-engineering of business processes. Development of project and process activity of the company is a mutually conditioned process.

Research limitations/implications In their research of the mutual conditionality of maturity of the project and process management, the authors have to rely largely on their research experience, because the process and project management maturity in the literature are reviewed separately.

Originality/value The paper's findings extend current knowledge. Its results provide guidance for scholars and practitioners involved in the design and implementation of enterprise architecture.

Paper type Research paper

Keywords Enterprise architecture • Business architecture • Process • Project • Maturity

I.V. Ilin (✉) • A.I. Lyovina
Saint Petersburg State Polytechnic University, Saint Petersburg, Russia
e-mail: isemfem@gmail.com

A.R. Antipin
Business Set Corp, Saint Petersburg, Russia

© Springer International Publishing Switzerland 2016   51
J. Becker et al. (eds.), *Emerging Trends in Information Systems*, Progress in IS,
DOI 10.1007/978-3-319-23929-3_5

1 Introduction

Effective management system is a key factor of business survival and success. To face business challenges appropriately companies try to build effective enterprise-wide management system that requires an integrated approach. The concept of the enterprise architecture as a complex management tool has become justly popular in recent decades.

One of the definitions states that *"enterprise architecture* is a coherent whole of principles, methods, and models that are used in the design and realization of an enterprise's organizational structure, business processes, information systems, and infrastructure" [1]. Traditionally, the enterprise architecture can be represented as a set of building blocks which are grouped into so called architecture layers, which are connected by means of services. The number and names of layers varies in different sources (for example [1–4]), but the concept is more or less the same. For example, [3] focuses on the following three layers:

- Corporate mission and vision, strategic goals and objectives
- Business architecture: business processes, organizational structure, workflow
- System Architecture (IT architecture): applications, data, hardware

Some researches justly confess the business architecture layer to be the primary element that shapes the effectiveness of the company [1, 5, 6]. In the meantime some authors [3, 4] do not outline explicitly within the business layer but mention in implicit way the need to introduce some management mechanism in addition to business processes which would allow to deal with changes and innovative activities. In Ref. [2] it is underlined that the enterprise architecture among other elements should include "transitional processes for implementing new technologies in response to the changing needs of the business". An answer to this request could be integrating a project management approach as a component of the business architecture. A *project* can be defined as "a temporary organization that is created for the purpose of delivering one or more business products" [7]. Project management as a management knowledge area takes place when the need to implement changes or realize unique activities appears. The model of enterprise architecture enriched with project management approach within business layer is presented on Fig. 1 [8].

The most important characteristic of the enterprise architecture is that it provides a holistic view of the enterprise [1]. Heterogeneous structure of the enterprise architecture requires continuous alignment of all its components. In the meantime, the need to follow the realities of today's business causes the need to reform and develop the enterprise architecture. While developing the enterprise architecture it is crucially important to keep aligning its layers and components within particular layers.

Nowadays companies have at their disposal a big variety of standards, guidelines and maturity models to improve the way they run business. However, most of these approaches are focused on a specific part of the enterprise architecture and do not

Fig. 1 Model of enterprise architecture layers [8]

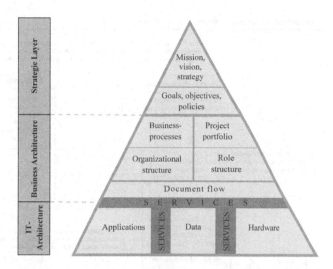

take a system approach to problems that most companies are facing. The focus of this paper is the development of business architecture by alignment and joint development of its components' maturity levels.

2 Business Process Management Maturity Models

Most of the researches agree that business process system is a key element of business architecture. The business process is "a special process that intends at the implementation of the basic objectives of the enterprise (business objectives) and describes the central sphere of its activity" [5]. The business processes as "a stable (regularly repeated), targeted set of interrelated activities, which according a certain technology transforms inputs into outputs which have value to the consumer (customer)" [6] define the organizational structure of the enterprise. The organizational structure is a stable set of interrelated and inter-subordinate organizational units to coordinate human resources of the company. "The process approach to management is a construction of a system of processes, control of these processes in order to achieve the best results, improving efficiency and customer satisfaction" [6]. In modern enterprises implementing process management involves description, regulation, updating, and improvement of business processes system and the organizational structure in order to ensure the stability and reproducibility of the results.

There are a lot of process maturity models—one of reviews is presented in Ref. [9]. One of the commonly used models is the Capability Maturity Model (CMM) and its successor Capability Maturity Model Integration (CMMI) developed by the Software Engineering Institute at Carnegie Mellon University. CMMI introduced the concept of five maturity levels defined by cumulative requirements. The certain number of models develop CMMI: Gartner's Process Maturity Model by Ref. [10],

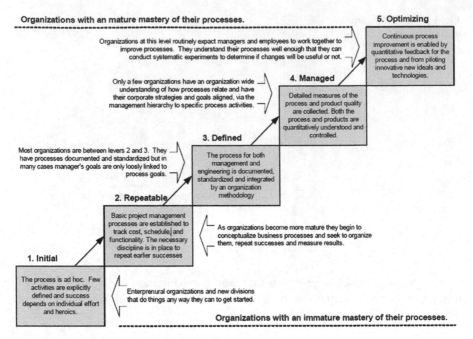

Fig. 2 Five maturity levels of CMMI model [15]

BPMM by Ref. [11], The Babson/Queensland University's Holistic BPM Maturity Model by Ref. [12], PEMM by Ref. [13].

Maturity levels according to Ref. [14] are used to characterize organizational improvement relative to a set of process areas, and capability levels characterize organizational improvement relative to an individual process area (Fig. 2).

3 Project Management Maturity Models

In 1997, [16] proposed a 5-level Project Management Process Maturity Model (also known as (PM)^2 model) to assess and improve an organization's current project management maturity level. The 5-Level (PM)^2 Model evolves from a functionally-driven organization to a project-driven organization. According to this model [16] the project management maturity levels are described as follows:

Level 1: Ad-hoc *stage.* There are no formal procedures or plans to execute a project. The project activities are poorly defined... PM processes are totally unpredictable and poorly controlled... Organizations at Level 1 are functionally isolated and are not familiar with the project management concept or the project-oriented organizational structure. A Level 1 organization can be described as trying to establish a basic project management process.

Level 2: Planned Stage. Informal and incomplete procedures manage a project... Project management processes are partially recognized and controlled by project managers. Nevertheless, planning and management of projects depend on individuals. The organization at Level 2 is more team-oriented than Level 1. The project's basic commitments are understood by the project team. This organization possesses a strength in doing similar and repeatable work. However, when the organization is presented with new and unfamiliar projects, the organization confronts major chaos in managing and controlling the project. Level 2 project management processes are efficient in individual project planning.

Level 3: Managed Stage. Project management processes become partially formal and demonstrate a basic project planning and control system. Most of the problems regarding project management are identified and informally documented for project control purpose... An organization at Level 3 concentrates on systematic and structured project planning and control. Project groups work together to manage the projects efficiently. People are trained to understand and to apply project management skills and practices. This organization works hard to integrate cross-functional teams to form a project team.

Level 4: Integrated Stage. Project management processes are formal and information and processes are documented. The organization at Level 4 can plan, manage, integrate, and control multiple projects efficiently. Project management processes are well defined, quantitatively measured, understood, and executed... A Level 4 organization can conduct multiple project planning and control.

Level 5: Sustained Stage. Project management processes are continuously improved. Problems associated with applying project management are fully understood and eliminated to ensure project success. The data collected is then rigorously analyzed and evaluated to select and to improve the project management processes. Organizations at Level 5 are involved in the continuous improvement of PM processes and practices. Each member of the project team spends efforts to maintain and to sustain the project-driven environment. Project teams are dynamic, energetic, and fluid to achieve project-oriented, project-centered organization.

Nowadays one of the most well-known project maturity models is P3M3 (which stands for Portfolio, Program and Project Management Maturity Model) originally developed by Office of Government Commerce, UK. According to Ref. [17], P3M3 uses a five-level maturity framework and the five Maturity Levels are: Level 1—awareness of process, Level 2—repeatable process, Level 3—defined process, Level 4—managed process, Level 5—optimized process. This maturity model allows for independent assessment in any of the specific disciplines—portfolio management, program management or project management—so it can be treated as 3 different model (Table 1) [17].

It is easy to notice that both project management maturity models are based on the quality of process management and project maturity levels are high-correlated with CMMI levels.

Table 1 Portfolio, programme and project management maturity models (P3M3) [17]

Maturity level	Portfolio management	Programme management	Project management
Level 1—awareness of process	Does the organization's Executive Board recognize programmes and projects, and maintain an informal list of its investments in programmes and projects? (There may be no formal tracking and documenting process)	Does the organization recognize programmes and run them differently from projects? (Programmes may be run informally with no standard process or tracking system)	Does the organization recognize projects and run them differently from its ongoing business? (Projects may be run informally with no standard process or tracking system)
Level 2—repeatable process	Does the organization ensure that each programme and/or project in its portfolio is run with its own processes and procedures to a minimum specified standard? (There may be limited consistency or coordination)	Does the organization ensure that each programme is run with its own processes and procedures to a minimum specified standard? (There may be limited consistency or coordination between programmes)	Does the organization ensure that each project is run with its own processes and procedures to a minimum specified standard? (There may be limited consistency or coordination between projects)
Level 3—defined process	Does the organization have its own centrally controlled programme and project processes and can individual programmes and projects flex within these processes to suit particular programmes and/or projects Does the organization have its own portfolio management process?	Does the organization have its own centrally controlled programme processes and an individual programmes flex within these processes to suit the particular programme?	Does the organization have its own centrally controlled project processes and can individual projects flex within these processes to suit the particular project?
Level 4—managed process	Does the organization obtain and retain specific management metrics on its whole portfolio of programmes and projects as a means of predicting future performance? Does the organization assess its capacity to manage programmes and projects and prioritize them accordingly?	Does the organization obtain and retain specific measurements on its programme management performance and run a quality management organization to better predict future performance?	Does the organization obtain and retain specific measurements on its project management performance and run a quality management organization to better predict future performance?
Level 5—optimized process	Does the organization undertake continuous process improvement with proactive problem	Does the organization undertake continuous process improvement with proactive problem	Does the organization undertake continuous process improvement with proactive problem

(continued)

Table 1 (continued)

Maturity level	Portfolio management	Programme management	Project management
	and technology management for the portfolio in order to improve its ability to depict performance over time and optimize processes?	and technology management for programmes in order to improve its ability to depict performance over time and optimize processes?	and technology management for projects in order to improve its ability to depict performance over time and optimize processes?

4 Business Architecture Maturity and Its Development

Maturity models in particular have become an essential tool in assessing organizations' current capabilities and helping them to implement change and improvements in a structured way. These models consist of a hierarchical collection of elements describing the characteristics of effective processes, and their use can enable organizations to reap the benefits brought by improved capability at all levels [17]. Business process and project management maturity models are traditionally used as a health check of the company or as a roadmap for future development of any particular management aspect (processes or projects). As key components of business architecture of the company, process and project management have a great impact on each other's maturity and on the business architecture maturity as a whole.

The design of enterprise architecture almost never starts with a blank sheet of paper, but instead involves the transformation of the enterprise from the as-is system architecture to the to-be system architecture. Moreover, this transformation takes place over the span of many years, and for some very large enterprises they may be constantly changing because they must survive and adapt in a constantly changing environment [18]. TOGAF features the Architecture Development Method (ADM), which is a comprehensive method for architecture. The ADM is a core component of the current version of TOGAF and ArchiMate provides a commentary on the use of different parts of the ArchiMate specification at different stages within the TOGAF ADM [19]. The transition from the current stable state of the enterprise architecture to the desired one can be described using the terminology of ArchiMate 2.0 modelling language (Fig. 3) [20]. Thus, to migrate from one plateau (a relatively stable state of the architecture) to the new one the company has to define the gap between them and develop a work package (a series of actions) to overcome it. The state of the architecture is defined by the states of its components. The latter factually is the maturity levels of these components (According to Ref. [21] "maturity levels characterize the overall state of organization's processes" or according to Ref. [22] "a maturity level is a defined evolutionary plateau for organizational process improvement").

Concepts and Relationships

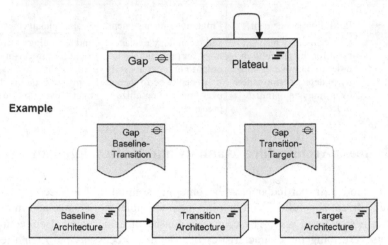

Example

Fig. 3 Migration viewpoint from implementation & migration extension, ArchiMate 2.0 modelling language [20]

In Ref. [23] the following components of the architecture process are mentioned:

- Build a baseline architecture that represents reality
- Build a target architecture that represents the business vision and IT strategies
- Develop a sequencing plan that describes an incremental strategy for transitioning the baseline to the target

Moving from one architecture plateau to another one, all architectural components should be treated as a system. That is why it seems critically important to take into account the phase of development (i.e. maturity level) of each component of the enterprise architecture and their correlation while developing architecture as a whole. If the company wants to develop its architecture, the following steps should be followed:

1. Describe the current state of the architecture including the maturity levels of its components
2. Describe the desired state of the architecture maturity and the maturity levels of its components needed to provide it
3. Develop a set of activities aimed to achieve the targeted maturity levels of architectural components which would provide the desired vision of the architecture state

According to the model proposed in Ref. [8] projects together with processes form the backbone of the business architecture. They define the organizational structure, the role structure and the document flow of the enterprise. Thus, the maturity level of the business architecture depends largely on the maturity of its key components.

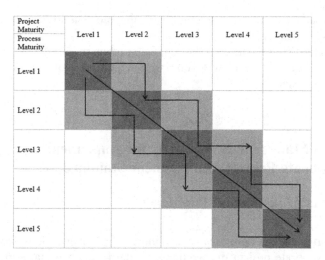

Fig. 4 Process and project management maturity matrix

In such a situation there cannot and should not be a significant gap between levels of development of these two components. Process and project maturity model analysis allows to create a 2-dimensional matrix of process and project maturity that helps to define the maturity of the whole business architecture (Fig. 4). Thus, process and project management are important components of enterprise management system, the relationship between maturities of these components is a key factor of business architecture development.

The business architecture can be considered as optimally-balanced if processes and projects are managed on the same level (dark-grey cells on Fig. 4). The business architecture can be called acceptably balanced in case of one-level difference between process and project management maturity levels (light-grey cells on Fig. 4). In such a case for further business architecture development it is reasonable to accumulate the capacity of the weaker component (in order to get into the dark-grey zone on Fig. 4). The path of sustainable development of business architecture is depicted with arrows on Fig. 4. The development can follow any of the arrows shown on Fig. 4 or any can be composed of different pieces of these arrows. The important note is that the development path lays within the grey area of the matrix.

The difference of more than one level between process and project dimensions of the matrix means that the enterprise has unbalances business architecture maturity model which prevents it from further development. If enterprise has higher process maturity level and wants to keep on with process management implementation it will need to establish a process reengineering project. It in turns will require project management skills of a certain level in order to deliver a necessary result. Thus, the right way would be to raise the project capacity first which will provide more effective moving towards new process maturity level. The reverse situation is a combination of higher project and lower process maturity levels. Project management is based on certain system of processes and the more sophisticated is a project approach adopted in the enterprise, the more serious requirements for process management are.

One of the business challenges where it is important to provide balanced system of process and project maturity levels is implementation of a corporate project management standard.

5 Process Management Maturity for Implementing a Corporate Project Management Standard

5.1 Project Management Standards

In order to run project activities in the most effective way it is reasonable to establish a corporate project management standard. It is especially important for so-called project-oriented companies—those whose main business is based on execution of 'projects for their customers. The single project management standard accepted in a company provides all the members of a project team with a common methods, tools and language while performing project activity.

The company can either develop its own project management approach or adopt one of the existing ones. The well-known project management approach within the world professional society are those developed by leading professional associations and organizations such as the Cabinet Office (United Kingdom), PMI (USA), Microsoft (USA), etc. The methodology of each approach is described in the guidelines—Managing Successful Projects Using PRINCE2 (Cabinet Office), PMBoK (PMI), MSF (Microsoft) correspondingly. Each approach claims to be the formalized result of analysis of the best practices in project management.

All of the standards address all major areas of project management (including cost, risk, quality, personnel management) from different points of view [7, 24, 25]. The basics of most project management standards are:

- Guideline
- Set of aspects that describe some certain sections of project management
- The system of business processes

Therefore, consideration of the project activity as a specifically organized system of business processes aimed to achieve certain goals:

- Sets a close link between process and project components of business architecture
- Defines processes as a primary component of business architecture
- Provides business architects with a single tool for modelling process and project activities based on process modelling approach

5.2 Modelling of Project Management Processes

As a methodological basis for a demonstration model of project management processes was chosen the PRINCE2 methodology (Fig. 5) because this standard reflects a structured approach to project management. This conclusion is based on the following characteristics PRINCE2:

- Systematic understanding of the project management process model with pre-scribed inputs, outputs, events that initiate the process
- Decomposition of the main processes (up to the third sub-level of decomposi-tion), representing a clear algorithm of project management at various manage-ment levels
- A clear definition of process owners ("roles and responsibilities" in terms of process management) for all project management processes
- Document flow system, which accompanies all processes of project manage-ment, and the availability of typical document templates

The landscape of business processes (processes of the first level of decomposi-tion) of project management prescribed by PRINCE2 are: Starting Up, Directing a Project, Initiating a Project, Controlling a Stage, Managing Product Delivery, Controlling a Stage Boundary, Closing a Project [7].

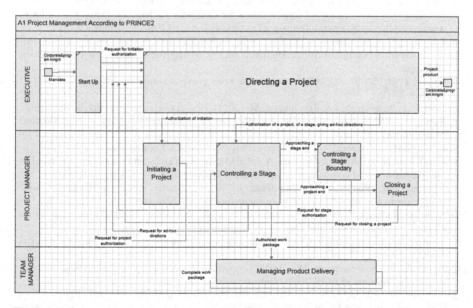

Fig. 5 Landscape of business processes of PRINCE2 project management standard [8]

6 Results and Discussions

Balanced enterprise architecture is based on the concept of the alignment. Traditionally the alignment means the balance between different architectural layers. But the alignment of the components of a particular layer is important as well, particularly the alignment between process and project maturity levels within the business architecture layer. The latter can be provided by the process approach to project management.

The transformation from the as-is architecture to the to-be one involves implementing the set of projects. The real options framework to plan a project portfolio for achieving a target architecture is described in [26]. The particular portfolio of projects intended to deliver a desired architecture capabilities depends on the current combination of process and project maturity levels. The description of typical projects needed to be implemented is a matter to investigate.

References

1. Lankhorst, M. (2013). *Enterprise architecture at work. Modelling, communication, analysis.* Berlin: Springer.
2. CIO Council. (2014, January 25). *Federal enterprise architecture framework version 1.1 September 1999.* Retrieved from Institute for Enterprise Architecture Development: http://www.enterprise-architecture.info/Images/Documents/Federal%20EA%20Framework.pdf
3. Kalyanov, G. (2014 January 25). *Enterprise architecture and instruments of its modeling.* Retrieved from National Institute Higher School of Management : http://www.vshu.ru/files/IR01a.pdf
4. Group, T. O. (2009). *TOGAF version 9. The open group architecture framework (TOGAF).* London: TSO.
5. Becker, J., Kugeler, M., & Rosenmann, M. (2011). *Process management.* Berlin: Springer.
6. Repin, V. (2013). *Business-processes. Modeling, implementation, management.* Moscow: Mann, Ivanov and Ferber.
7. OGC. (2009). *Managing successful projects with PRINCE2.* London: TSO.
8. Ilin, I. V., Antipin, A. R., & Lyovina, A. I. (2013). Business architecture modeling for process- and project-oriented companies. *Economics and Management, 95,* 32–38.
9. Röglinger, M., Pöppelbuß, J., & Becker, J. (2012). Maturity models in business process management. *Business Process Management Journal, 18,* 328–346.
10. Scott, D., Pultz, J. E., Holub, E., Bittman, T. J., & McGuckin, P. (2007). *Introducing the Gartner IT infrastructure and operations.* Stamford: Gartner.
11. Object Management Group. (2008). *Business process maturity model (BPMM). Version 1.0.* OMG.
12. De Bruin, T., & Rosemann, M. (2005). *Towards a business process management maturity model* (Proceedings of ECIS 2005). Germany: Regensburg.
13. Hammer, M. (2007, April). The process audit. *Harvard Business Review,* 111–123.
14. Software Engineering Institute. (2010). *CMMI® for development, version 1.3.* Carnegie Mellon University.
15. Chrissis, M. B., Konrad, M., & Shrum, S. (2003). *CMMI: Guidelines for process integration and product development.* Reading, MA: Addison-Wesley.

16. Kwak, Y. H., & Ibbs, W. C. (2002, July). Project management process maturity (PM2) model. *Journal of Management in Engineering*, 150–155.
17. AXELOS. (2014, January 25). *Portfolio, programme and project management (P3M3). Introduction and guide to P3M3*. Retrieved from P3M3 Official Site: http://www.p3m3-officialsite.com/P3M3Model/Model_mhtry.aspx
18. Giachetti, R. E. (2010). *Design of enterprise systems: Theory, architecture, and methods*. Boca Raton, FL: CRC Press.
19. Jonkers, H., Proper, E., & Turner, M. (2009). *TOGAF™ and ArchiMate®: A future together. A vision for convergence & co-existence*. The Open Group.
20. The Open Group. (2012). *A pocket guide to ArchiMate 2.0*. The Open Group.
21. CMMI Product Team. (2010). *CMMI® for development, version 1.3*. Carnegie Mellon University.
22. Trinity Management Consultants Limited. (2014, February 01). *Overview of maturity levels*. Retrieved from Trinity Management Consultants Limited: http://www.trinity-cmmi.co.uk/TR/Maturity-Levels.htm
23. CIO Council. (2001). *A practical guide to federal enterprise architecture*. Chief Information Officer Council.
24. PMI. (2013). *A guide to the project management body of knowledge: PMBOK guide*. 5th ed. Project Management Institute.
25. Turner, M. (2006). *Microsoft® solutions framework essentials: Building successful technology solutions*. Microsoft Press.
26. Giachetti, R. E. (2012). A flexible approach to realize an enterprise architecture. *Procedia Computer Science, 8*, 147–152.

Algorithms for Project Portfolio Selection Based on Fuzzy Multi-objective Model

Alexey A. Lifshits and Sergey M. Avdoshin

Abstract The companies that are IT-industry leaders perform from several tens to several hundreds of projects simultaneously. The main problem is to decide whether the project is acceptable to the current strategic goals and resource limits of a company or not. This leads firms to an issue of a project portfolio selection; therefore, the challenge is to choose the subset of all projects which satisfy the strategic objectives of a company in the best way. In this present article we propose the multi-objective mathematical model of the project portfolio selection problem, defined on the fuzzy trapezoidal numbers. We provide an overview of methods for solving this problem, which are a branch and bound approach, an adaptive parameter variation scheme based on the epsilon-constraint method, ant colony optimization method and genetic algorithm. After analysis, we choose ant colony optimization method and SPEA II method, which is a modification of a genetic algorithm. We describe the implementation of these methods applied to the project portfolio selection problem. The ant colony optimization is based on the max min ant system with one pheromone structure and one ant colony. Three modification of our SPEA II implementation were considered. The first adaptation uses the binary tournament selection, while the second requires the rank selection method. The last one is based on another variant of generating initial population. The part of the population is generated by a non-random manner on the basis of solving a one-criterion optimization problem. This fact makes the population more strongly than an initial population, which is generated completely by random.

Keywords Project portfolio • Multi-objective model • Fuzzy numbers • Genetic algorithm • Ant colony optimization

A.A. Lifshits • S.M. Avdoshin (✉)
Software Management Department, School of Software Engineering, National Research University Higher School of Economics, Moscow, Russia
e-mail: savdoshin@hse.ru

© Springer International Publishing Switzerland 2016
J. Becker et al. (eds.), *Emerging Trends in Information Systems*, Progress in IS,
DOI 10.1007/978-3-319-23929-3_6

65

1   Introduction

The companies that are IT-industry leaders perform from several tens to several hundreds of projects simultaneously. And projects can respond to various strategic objectives of the company. Following [1], under the project, we consider the unique set of processes, including manageable tasks, start and finish dates, undertaken to achieve a specific goal.

Frequently, projects are not consider the company's mission and strategic goals that can be not directly related to the main activity of the company, such as an increase in the competitiveness of the market, development of new technologies, etc. As a result, the situation may arise when profitable projects which do not meet the company's goals, exceed less profitable projects, albeit fully meet the strategic goals of the company. According to statistics [2], only about 20 % of management initiatives designed to monitor the implementation of the strategic objectives are realized. For solving the problem of strategic goals accounting the project portfolio management process is introduced. Here, under the project portfolio we consider a set of independent projects, which are realized according to the resources constraints and satisfied company strategic objectives in a certain way [2].

The aim of this work is solving the problem of projects portfolio selection, which is the first step in the process of project portfolio management. In this case, firstly, it is necessary to formalize a mathematical model of the problem, and secondly, to choose the most effective methods for solving this problem.

The mathematical model should consider various strategic goals of a company and different types of resources.

To decide whether it is possible to include a project into a portfolio, it is necessary to provide an initial assessment of its corresponding to strategy goals and required resources. However, in the early stages it is virtually impossible to determine the exact numerical values of the parameters of specific projects as organizations do not have accurate information about financial flows and resource costs. To forecast these indicators different methods, which involves experts' opinions can be used. Typically the final assessment of the financial indicators consists of three numbers: the minimum, the maximum and the most likely estimate. To evaluate linguistic (non-financial) indicators of the project (for example, the degree of technological innovation), also three indicators can be used: minimum (the least favorable), maximum (the most favorable) and the most probable. Thus, the presentation of data as three estimates is convenient and allows taking into account boundary scenarios of project development. In the case if mathematical model of the problem of project portfolio can use only standard data, it is possible to consider the most probable estimate or some aggregated values, taking into account all three estimates. It is possible to note that in the case of choosing the most probable estimate or the aggregate value, the part of data is lost, and this fact may adversely affect the accuracy of the obtained solutions.

The presence of multi-criteria aspect of goal-setting, allows us to formulate the task of forming a balanced portfolio, taking into account the various objectives of the organization. Solution is the set of possible portfolios and the final choice can be done by system analysis methods (for instance analytic hierarchy process).

2   Mathematical Models

2.1   Review of Existing Models

In work [3], a multi-criteria model of portfolio with one restriction is proposed. In the first step, the authors suggest to perform evaluation of projects by experts. As a result each project is assigned one of three categories: priority, satisfactoriness and acceptability, and within each the groups of projects are sorted according to the level of compliance. For the model, the authors suggest using 6 objective functions: the number of projects in a possible solution for each of three groups, the total number of projects, and for priority categories and satisfactory—estimates based on the extent of compliance. Also the authors take into account the company budget constraint.

Lean Yu considers in his paper [4] a single-criterion model. The objective function consists of two parts: the first part is an estimate of the effect of independent projects (for each project the calculation of a weighted sum of a project compliance to company goals is performed), and the second is based on the effect of the joint implementation of several projects. The number of projects in the portfolio is set as the limitation of the model.

2.2   Proposed Mathematical Model

We introduce the following variables:

- N—set of available projects, $|N| = n$
- M—set of resources, $|M| = m$
- K—set of criteria (strategic company goals), $|K| = k$
- Q—project portfolio, $|Q| = q$, $Q \subseteq N$,

In this work we will identify the set of projects, resources and criteria with the set of their numbers.

A project i, $i \in N$, is characterized by:

- Goals satisfaction vector

$$a_i = (a_{1i}, a_{2i}, \ldots, a_{ki}),$$

where a_{il}—numerical characteristic of satisfaction criterion l in project i, $l \in K$

- Required resources vector

$$c_i = (c_{1i}, c_{2i}, \ldots, c_{mi}),$$

where c_{ji}—the need of resources $j, j \in M$ for implementation of project i

Project portfolio Q is characterized by:

- Goals satisfaction vector

$$a_Q = (a_{1Q}, a_{2Q}, \ldots, a_{kQ}), where\ a_{lQ} = \sum_{i=1}^{q} a_{li},\ l \in K$$

- Required resources vector

$$c_Q = (c_{1Q}, c_{2Q}, \ldots, c_{mQ}), where\ c_{jQ} = \sum_{i=1}^{q} c_{ji},\ j \in M.$$

Here we assume the presence of the addictiveness principle of projects esti-
mations, according to which the portfolio goals satisfaction vector and portfolio
required resources vector are equal to the sum of the corresponding vectors of
projects, included in the portfolio. Another assumption is that in this model we do
not consider the relationship between projects and possible common effect of
realizing projects.

Company resource constraints are given by the vector of resource constraints,
which we denote as R, where $R = (R1, R2, \ldots, Rm)$. Thus, projects portfolios have to
satisfy an inequality $c_Q \leq R$ componentwise.

It is required to maximize the degree of compliance with company strategic
goals.

$$\begin{cases} \sum_{i=1}^{N} a_{1i}x_i \rightarrow max \\ \quad \ldots \\ \sum_{i=1}^{N} a_{li}x_i \rightarrow max \\ \quad \ldots \\ \sum_{i=1}^{N} a_{ki}x_i \rightarrow max \end{cases} \tag{1}$$

$$\sum_{i=1}^{N} c_{ji}x_i \leq Rj,\ j \in M$$

Here $x_i \in \{0,1\}$, $x_i = 1$, if the project i is included into a portfolio and $x_i = 0$,
otherwise.

The components of goals satisfaction vector, required resources vector and company resource constraints vector are specified using trapezoidal fuzzy numbers. This fact allows to take into consideration the possible lack of information at an early stage.

Fuzzy trapezoidal number A is determined by the membership function $\mu_A:R \to$ [0,1] which is defined as follows:

$$\mu_A(x) = \begin{cases} 0, & x\langle a1 \text{ или } x\rangle a4 \\ \dfrac{x-a1}{a2-a1}, & a1 \leq x < a2 \\ 1, & a2 \leq x \leq a3 \\ \dfrac{a4-x}{a4-a3}, & a3 < x \leq a4 \end{cases} \tag{2}$$

Hence, trapezoidal fuzzy number is defined by four parameters ranked in ascending $a1, a2, a3, a4$.

It is possible to notice that the addition and subtraction operations are internal binary operations specified on the set of parametrically defined trapezoidal fuzzy numbers. Thus, you can perform calculations on such numbers without changing their representation [5].

2.3   Model Comparison

Model [3] is based on sorting of projects in relation to each other and does not take into consideration possible quantitative results of the project (net present value, internal rate of return). This may adversely affect the resulting portfolios of projects.

As a disadvantage of model [4] it is possible to point out one objective function that makes the result strongly dependent on the choice of weights. The next drawback is the lack of consideration of company resource constraints.

We present comparative characteristics of the analysis results (Table 1).

Based on the comparative analysis we can conclude that the proposed mathematical model considers a number of important factors of portfolio selection problem, which proves the practical significance of the proposed model.

Table 1 Comparative analysis of project portfolio selection models

Model	Number of objective functions	Number of constraints	Possibility of fuzzy estimations	Solution format	Dependencies between projects considered
Model [2]	6	1	no	Set of possible portfolios	No
Model [3]	1	1	no	A project portfolio	Yes
Proposed model	Not limited	Not limited	yes	Set of possible portfolios	No

3 Solution Methods

3.1 Review of Existing Methods

Discussed in this section approaches have been used to solve the problem without the use of fuzzy numbers.

The simplest one is brute force method [2], which is an adaptation of branch and bound approach. Asymptotic complexity of this method is $O(2^n)$, where $n = |N|$.

Adaptive parameter variation scheme based on epsilon-constraint method [6] allows determining the Pareto optimal solutions based on the results obtained from solving single-criterion optimization problems. It determines the optimal resource constraint on iteration. Asymptotic complexity of this method is $O(k^{m-1} * T)$, where k—number of found Pareto-optimal solutions, m—number of goals, and T—complexity of solving a single-criterion optimization problem.

Ant colony optimization. This method is inspired by the behavior of an ant's colony. At the beginning ants move randomly, and after finding food return to their colony while laying down pheromone trails. If other ants find such a path, they are likely not to keep travelling at random, but to follow the trail, returning and reinforcing it if they eventually find food. Also over time, the amount of pheromone decreases. Possible paths are represented as a pheromone structure, where projects are vertexes of the graph and amount of pheromones are values on edges. At the end of iteration edges, which were part of the Pareto-optimal solutions of generation, are updated [7].

Genetic algorithm. The algorithm is based on an evolutionary technique; population consists of individuals that are possible solutions. Each individual stores data in the genotype and the phenotype. In this case, the genotype of individuals is the bit string of ones and zeros, indicating whether is a project included to the current solution or not. The phenotype is interpreted in two portfolio vectors: the resource constraints vector and goals satisfaction vector. In this work we provide the modification of SPEA II, which is one of the best genetic algorithms for solving multi-objective problems [8]. The asymptotic complexity of one iteration of algorithm is $O(m^3)$, where m—the total number of individuals in archive and generation.

3.2 Methods Selection

For solving this problem the ant colony optimization algorithm and the SPEA II modification were selected as they have better asymptotic complexity than the brute force method and the modification of epsilon-constraint method.

3.3 Ant Colony Optimization

In this paper we propose the modification of max min ant colony system based on the algorithm outlined in [7]. The overall structure of the algorithm is follows:

1. Pheromone structure initialization.

   Each edge in pheromone structure graph is initialized by the predefined value τ_{max}.
2. For each ant we build solution.
3. Pheromone structure update.

   Pareto dominated possible solutions are deleted and the edges on the structure of pheromones, which are included in the remaining possible solutions, are updated. Values of all edges between nodes in this possible solutions are increased by a fixed value τ_{upd}.
4. Constraint satisfaction checking on the edges of the pheromones structure.

$$\text{If } \tau_{cur} > \tau_{max}, \ \tau_{cur} = \tau_{max}.$$
$$\text{If } \tau_{cur} > \tau_{min}, \ \tau_{cur} = \tau_{min}.$$

5. If the specified number of iterations is not exceeded, move to step 2, otherwise finish the algorithm.

We define a Pareto dominance relation: portfolio A dominates portfolio B, if at least one of the criteria of A is better, and the remaining criteria are not worse than B's criteria.

Let us consider the step 2, and show how to create a solution for each agent (ant) in relation to project portfolio selection problem.

1. Sets initialization:

$$S = \varnothing. \ \text{Cand} = V;$$

$R^* = R$, where V—a set of projects, R—company resources constraints, and S—projects, included in the ant path.

2. Termination checking:
   If Cand$= \varnothing$, then solution is built.
3. Solution adding:
   Select $v_i \in C$ and with the probability $p_s(v_i)$;

$$S = S + \{v_i\}.$$

4. Parameters update:
   Cand $=$ Cand$-\{v_i\}$;

$$R_j^* = R_j^* - c_{jv_i}, \ j = 1, \ldots, m,$$

   where c_{jv_i}—resource requirements of type j of project v_i.
5. Resources constraints violation checking R_j^*:
   Projects from the set Cand, which violate the current resources constraints, are removed.
6. Move to step 2.

Next, we consider the method of calculating the probability with which an ant chooses the next project among possible.

The probability $p_s(v_i)$ for each agent is calculated as follows:

$$p_s(v_i) = \frac{[\tau_S^{R^*}(v_i)]^{\alpha} * [\sigma_S^{R^*}(v_i)]^{\beta}}{\sum_{v_j \in Cand} [\tau_S^{R^*}(v_j)]^{\alpha} * [\sigma_S^{R^*}(v_j)]^{\beta}}, \tag{3}$$

where $\tau_S^{R^*}(v_i)$ –pheromone factor, a $\sigma_S^{R^*}(v_i)$—heuristic factor.

Pheromone factor is calculated based on the structure of pheromones:

$$\tau_S^{R^*}(v_i) = \sum_{v_j \in S} \tau(v_i, v_j).$$

That is the sum by the number of pheromones, lying on the edges of the compounds of this project with the already selected by the current ant projects.

Heuristic factor is calculated as follows:

1. Power factor of the remaining resources:

$$h_S^{R^*}(v_i) = \sum_{j=1}^{m} \frac{c_{ji}}{R_j^*},\qquad(4)$$

where R_j^*—the remaining amount of the resource j and c_{ji}—amount of the required resource j of project i.

2. Total heuristic factor:

$$\sigma_S^{R^*}(v_i) = \frac{a_i}{h_S^{R^*}(v_i)},\qquad(5)$$

where a_i—randomly chosen goal of project i.

3.4 Genetic Algorithm

The proposed alternative algorithm for solving project portfolio selection problem is based on the general scheme of the genetic algorithm SPEA II [8].

1. Initialization of the population and the archive.
2. Generation of the initial population.
3. Calculation of the fitness functions for the current population and an archive.
4. Selection and placing the best solutions in the archive (archive truncation if necessary).
5. Termination if the specified number of iterations is exceeded.
6. Crossover and mutation
7. Creation of a new generation and the transition to step 3.

The algorithm for the calculation of the fitness function consists of several steps:

1. Calculation of the solution "strength" as the number of solutions which are dominated by this chromosome:

$$S_i = |\{j \,|\, j \in P_t + P_t^- \cap i >_{Pareto} j\}|,\qquad(6)$$

where $i = 1,\ldots,n$, $+-$ union of sets and $>_{Pareto}$ demonstrates Pareto dominance.
2. Based on S_i, a fitness indicator is calculated, showing the number of solutions that dominates the current solution.

$$R_i = \sum_{j \in P_t + P_t^- , \; j >_{Pareto} i} S_j,\qquad(7)$$

where $i = 1,\ldots,n$
3. Calculation of δ_i (a distance to k-neighbor, where $k = \sqrt{N + N^-}$), where N—population size, and N^-—archive size.

4. Calculation of solution density:

$$D_i = 1 \Big/ {\delta_i + 2}$$ (8)

5. The resulting fitness function:

$$F_i = R_i + D_i,$$ (9)

In this case the fitness function tends to be minimized.

As each individual represents a possible portfolio of projects, it is possible to define the algorithm for calculating the phenotype applied to the project portfolio selection problem.

1. Initialize the vector of required resources and vector of objectives satisfaction with empty values:
   $Res = \varnothing$. where Res—vector of required resources for an individual (a possible portfolio);
   $Goal = \varnothing$. where $Goal$—vector of objectives satisfaction for an individual (a possible portfolio).
2. For each project i, $i \in N$.
3. Check, whether the selected project is included into the genotype of individual, and if yes, then move to step 4, otherwise choosing next project.
4. Perform parameters update:

$$Res = Res + a_i;$$
$$Goal = Goal + c_i.$$

5. Check the satisfaction of constraints R:
   If $Res < = R$, then choose next project, else move to step 6.
6. Start randomly selecting a project from the list of all possible projects until project that belongs to this individual wasn't chosen. Remove it from the genotype of the individual and go to step 1.

Consider the following mechanisms of selecting individuals: rank selection and binary tournament selection.

Rank selection. It consists of several actions:

1. All solutions are sorted.
2. Worst decision is assigned the rank 1, the next—2, and so on.
3. An individual is selected with the fixed probability pi / total, where pi is the rank of a given individual, and total is the sum of the ranks of all individuals.

Binary tournament selection. This function consists of the following steps:

1. Randomly choose two individuals from the population.
2. These individuals are compared by the values of its fitness function.

3. Individual with a lower value (the best in the context of the project portfolio selection problem) is selected with the fixed probability p (p > 80 %). Another individual is selected, respectively, with probability 1–p.

In the standard approach of the initial population generation, an individual's genotype is created by random. This leads to the fact that solutions obtained from the first iteration of the algorithm have a small phenotype value. We propose a method of generating an initial population in which some individual's genotype is set by a nonrandom manner. After solving a single-criterion problem for each criterion, we get individuals that Pareto dominates the majority of randomly generated individuals. In addition, we use a greedy algorithm to solve a single-criterion problem with many constraints [9].

4   Numerical Experiments

Numerical experiments for identifying the most efficient algorithm were performed over standard (non-fuzzy) model, since the use of fuzziness equally affects each of the methods.

Let us compare the speed of execution of algorithms depending on the number of projects. In the experiments, the test objects were created from the 100, 250 and 500 projects, with three goals and five constraints (Table 2).

According to this table, we can conclude that ant colony optimization shows a strong dependence on the number of projects and under a significant number of projects is inefficient, requiring considerable amount of time, even for 250 projects seriously losing to the genetic algorithm modifications. These, in turn, depend weakly on the total number of projects, showing about the same time.

Also we perform pair-wise comparisons of algorithms based on the calculated C-metric [7]. For two solution sets X' and X'', C-metric is calculated as follows:

Table 2 Speed of execution

Algorithm	Execution speed, % (relatively SPEA-II (binary tournament selection))		
	100 projects	250 projects	500 projects
Ant colony optimization	200	1800	15,900
SPEA-II (binary tournament selection)	100	100	100
SPEA-II (rank selection)	102	101	100
SPEA-II (strong initial population)[a]	104	102	103

[a]In this implementation a mechanism of rank selection was used

Table 3 C-metric

Algorithm	Average C-metric		
	100 projects	250 projects	500 projects
SPEA-II (binary tournament selection), SPEA-II (rank selection)	(0,21;0,19)	(0,23;0,18)	(0,31;0,54)
SPEA-II (binary tournament selection), SPEA-II (strong initial population)	(0,2;0,21)	(0,18;0,21)	(0,04;0,67)
SPEA-II (rank selection), SPEA-II (strong initial population)	(0,21;0,23)	(0,17;0,21)	(0;0,97)
Ant colony optimization, SPEA-II (strong initial population)	(0;1)	(0;1)	(0;1)

$$C\left(X', X''\right) = \frac{\left|\{a'' \in X'' : \exists \, a' \in X', \, a' >_{Pareto} a''\}\right|}{|X''|}. \tag{10}$$

For instance if $C\left(X', X''\right) = 1$, all solutions from the set X'' are dominated by the solutions from the set X'.

We perform pair-wise algorithms comparisons based on the average C-metric for 10 runs. In brackets in the table cells are $C\left(X', X''\right)$ and $C\left(X'', X'\right)$, where X'—solution set of the algorithm, which specified first in the corresponding table columns, and X''—specified second (Table 3).

Having considered this table, we can see that genetic algorithms demonstrate similar results for the 100 and 250 projects with a slight advantage of algorithm based on strong initial population. However, this modification is almost completely dominated the other algorithms with randomly generated initial population on 500 projects. Also it overcomes ant colony optimization. Thus, for solving project portfolio selection problem algorithm based on strong initial population can be considered as one of the optimal ones.

5   Summary

In the article the project portfolio selection problem was presented and its current relevance was justified. A brief description of existing models was introduced and the final multi-objective mathematical problem was formulated. Also an extension of the model using fuzzy sets for considering the inaccuracy of earlier projects indicators was described. We conducted a review of existing methods for solving multi-objective optimization problem, and as a result ant colony optimization method and genetic algorithm were chosen to implement, because of its asymptotic complexity.

Implementation of the genetic algorithm is based on SPEA II and we present three modifications of this algorithm that have different selection mechanism and function for initial population generation. The conducted experiments show that running time of ant colony optimization algorithm significantly increases with the number of projects, which makes it considerably slower compared with the modifications of the genetic algorithm if the number of projects is more than 250. And the genetic algorithm based on strong initial population surpasses the other presented algorithms and tends to be one of the most efficient algorithms for solving project portfolio selection problem.

References

1. International Standardization Organization. *Project management in accordance with ISO 21500*. Retrieved from July 2013 http://iso21500.ru/
2. Matveev, A., Novikov, D., & Tsvetkov, A. (2004). *Models and methods of project portfolio management*. Moscow: PMSOFT [in Russian].
3. Bastiani, S., Cruz, L., Fernandez, E., Gómez, C., & Ruiz, V. (2013). Project ranking-based portfolio selection using evolutionary multiobjective optimization of a vector proxy impact measure. In *Proceedings of the Eureka fourth international workshop*. Mazatlan, Mexico.
4. Yu, L., Wang, S., Wen, F., & Lai, K. (2012). Genetic algorithm-based multi-criteria project portfolio selection. *Annals of Operations Research, 197*(1), 71–86.
5. Anshin, V., Dyomkin, I., Tsarkov, I., & Nikonov, I. (2008). On application of fuzzy set theory to the problem of project portfolio selection. *Issues of risk analysis, 3*(5), 8–21 [in Russian].
6. Zitzler, E., Laumanns, M., & Thiele, L. (2006). An efficient, adaptive parameter variation scheme for metaheuristics based on the epsilon-constraint method. *European Journal of Operational Research, 169*(3), 932–942.
7. Alaya, I., Solnon, C., & Ghedira, K. (2007). Ant colony optimization for multi-objective optimization problems. In *Proceedings of the 19th IEEE international conference on tools with artificial intelligence* (Vol. 1, pp. 450–457). Patras, Greece.
8. Zitzler, E., Laumanns, M., & Thiele, L. (2001). *SPEA2: Improving the strength pareto evolutionary algorithm*. Technical report 103, Zurich: ETH
9. Akcay, Y., Li, H., & Xu, S. (2007). Greedy algorithm for the general multidimensional knapsack problem. *Annals of Operations Research, 150*(1), 17–29.

Advancement of Information Competencies in Training a New Generation of Economists

Safiullin Azat, Strelnik Evgenia, and Ushakova Tatiana

Abstract High quality training of the specialists working in the information sphere has become an important driver in successful development of the economy and the society. Expectations of the employers towards employees' information competencies are changing simultaneously with the public, social and technological progress. Competence approach focuses at the result of the education gained—a person's ability to act in various situations. This study about the level of training of economists in the field of information technology in the Russian universities.

Keywords Training process of the bachelors in economics • Core information competencies • Parallel accounting • Optimization and performance of the improvement of the efficiency of budgeting and project activities

Information technologies promote the improvement of business efficiency and the quality of life of the citizens. Computerization of business and society contributes to:

– Acceleration of business processes and integration of information technology
– Reduction of the levels of administrative hierarchy and cross-functional barriers in management with a view to improve the transparency of decision- making
– Optimization of production costs and timing synchronization of the production process
– Organization of the projects relevant to branch characteristics and market trends
– Development of innovative technology's projects which can qualitatively transform business processes at the enterprises and provide strategic competitive advantages

Fundamental changes in the economy, jobs, and businesses have reshaped workplaces and the nature of work. Over the last several decades, the industrial economy based on manufacturing has shifted to a service economy which is driven by information, knowledge, innovation and creativity [1].

S. Azat (✉) • S. Evgenia • U. Tatiana
Kazan (Volga Region) Federal University, 18 Kremlyovskaya St., 420008 Kazan, Republic of Tatarstan, Russian Federation
e-mail: safiullin.ar@gmail.com

© Springer International Publishing Switzerland 2016 79
J. Becker et al. (eds.), *Emerging Trends in Information Systems*, Progress in IS,
DOI 10.1007/978-3-319-23929-3_7

Thus, the demand for human resources who can be capable of developing an innovative capacity through integration of new information technologies and information systems has been dramatically increasing.

High quality training of the specialists working in the information sphere has become an important driver in successful development of the economy and the society. One of the most important tasks in training specialists in line with current renovation of the university education in Russia is mastering information competencies. Results of empirical researches indicate that investing in staff training organization of oil and gas sector, healthcare and defense industry most actively [2].

Designing the learning technologies in creating information competence of the Bachelors in Economics comprises the following respective steps:

- The research of labor market requirements
- The determination of the nomenclature of the specialties
- The identification of requirements to the specialists
- The state educational standards of higher education
- The contents of the information component of the training process of the Bachelors in Economics
- The professional activity of the graduates

Competence approach focuses at the result of the education gained—a person's ability to act in various situations. These situations are defined by the features of the profession.

For example, according to the professional standard "Management (leadership) organization" the key competencies of professional managers are the following:

8 D.2. To create conditions for ongoing changes and innovations within the organization;
6 B 6. To conduct of the projects' / processes' flow;
6 D.4. To lead changes and innovations;
6 E.2 To implement optimization of the projects / processes;
5/2 B.12 To develop proposals on optimization of industrial and economic activity;
5/2 E.3 To upgrade the processes and the technology under the organization's units [3].

In addition to the professional knowledge in economics, the economists should know information technology, and master computer and economic data analysis skills employed in the field of their professional activity.

The general requirements for skilled economic profile are the following: participation in the budgeting system, monitoring of budget execution, document preparation and formation of periodic and management reports, economic support of the company (net cost calculation, economic indicators for management decision-making preparation, etc.).

A number of studies shows that Russian employers in the list of "core information competencies" put main emphasis on competence-related knowledge of the basic methods, ways and means of production, storage, information processing; presence of computer skills, and ability to work with modern means of communication as well as in the global computer networks within the management of information. The professional activity of economists includes observation and research work, collection and analysis of data, monitoring of the economic trends and development the forecasts. All these professional competences require a combination of mastering the universal information management skills with mastering relevant professional software products [4].

State educational standards of higher education in the field of "Economics and Management" have the following components: "Economics", "Management", "Personnel Management", "Business Informatics", "State and municipal manage-ment." The most popular high school level training is "Economics" and "Business Informatics".

We consider the most important elements of information competence in training specialists in Economics to be the following:

- An understanding of information objects and their transformation by means of information technology, of hardware and software implementing these technologies
- A complex of general educational and professional knowledge and the skills based on processing and use of information, etc...

Based on these criteria we conducted a review of training programs for the Bachelors of Economics of some Russian federal and regional universities.

We examined the training programs of Chuvash State University, Samara State University, Samara State Economic University, Mari State University, Southern Federal University, and Urals Federal University.

As a result of the research we came to the following conclusion: all universities without a status of "federal" include minimum number of academic disciplines that develop the information competencies of the Bachelors in Economics in their training programs. Most universities add to their training programs academic disciplines recommended by the Ministry of Education. Their content is different from each other significantly. For example, one of the universities' teaching course "Business Informatics" do not have such a didactic unit as "erp-system" in the training program. The ways of solving tasks in MS Excel and in some cases the solution of practical tasks within 1C software product are considered within the course "Information systems in Economics" [5].

Our research also showed that those federal universities, which have an oppor-tunity to build their own educational standards, form the list of teaching programs which consider greater number of information competencies. Moreover, students can choose more disciplines associated with mathematics and natural sciences. However, the research did not reveal the facts of practical training of the econo-mists in the field of corporate information systems.

Teaching of the main educational programs should carry out such professional competences in the field of information technology as:

- Implementation of modern technology and information technology for solving communication tasks [6]

- Expertise in the method of project management and readiness to implement the project using modern software
- Knowledge the means of software analysis and quantitative modeling of control systems

Expectations of the employers towards employees' information competencies are changing simultaneously with the public, social and technological progress. The most urgent practical problems of business that can be solved with the help of modern information technologies are maintenance and formation a parallel accounting, consolidation of reports of a group of companies, conducting of a parallel tax accounting, optimization and performance of the improvement of the efficiency of budgeting and project activities. We propose to examine the possibility of developing tasks within SAP UA products for a financial direction, budgeting and project activities separately. The Institute of Management, Economics and Finance KFU is ready to participate in the development of such educational studies, and ensure their inclusion into their basic curricula of Bachelor's economic profile.

It is fruitful to highlight the regional dimension of information technology. Significant work has been implementing in performing information systems and communication technologies in public administration in the Republic of Tatarstan. Such projects are aimed at providing governmental information openness, increasing the efficiency of interaction of the state governance structures, business and society, creating the most comfortable conditions for the provision of a wide range of services of the population of the Republic of Tatarstan.

In Tatarstan along with other Russian regions there is an acute shortage of qualified personnel who are able to engage effectively in the organization of complex information systems in business and public administration, and to work as organizers of corporate information systems. Kazan Federal University made a major step forward in training such specialists for Tatarstan and other regions of the Privolzhsky Federal District through joint efforts of the Institute of Economics and Finance, Institute of Computational Mathematics and Information Technology and the Higher School of ITIS. The human capacity and logistical support of these units KFU meet all necessary requirements.

Kazan (Volga Region) Federal University was included in the list of the government support aimed at moving into the top one hundred of the world ranking of universities along with other leading Russian universities. KFU prepared a program for improving competitiveness, where information technologies constitute one of the priorities for the coming years. The target model of University's roadmap of increasing competitiveness is based on the analysis of the referent universities and forecasts research directions. Roadmap consists of 10 major components, which constitute a KPI system. Modernization of information systems and its internalization is an important element of the target model Institute of Economics and Finance KFU for 2013–2020 indicates the following activities under the roadmap to improve the quality of multidisciplinary training of economists [7]:

1. Development of joint educational programs with foreign partners. Determination of the total set of necessary resource support for the educational programs (technical

equipment, information resources, practice bases, etc.). Involvement of the world's leading specialists to the development and review of the educational content.

2. Localization of the best educational programs of universities TOP-200 (translation and adaptation of the text content and interfaces of electronic educational resources; transfer / duplication of audio and video materials, adaptation topics papers and control procedures).

3. Development and implementation in the Institute of Economics and Finance KFU Master, postgraduate and doctoral programs of world level. Attraction leading foreign scientists to implement graduate programs to the leadership doctoral and PhD programs.

4. Professional development of KFU professors in the world's leading universities.

5. Development of procedures for an international projects' expertise carried out at the Institute of Economics and Finance KFU. Creation of the expert council with the participation of scientists from leading research centers and experts from leading companies.

6. Implementation of the program "Personalized research centers." Attraction leading foreign experts to the leadership collaborative projects, laboratories, and in the structure of Institute of Economics and Finance KFU.

7. Creation in the Institute of Economics and Finance KFU basic chairs of the leading companies.

Economics and Finance Institute at KFU is ready to consider all possible options for cooperation in the framework of SAP University Alliances to achieve their goals.

References

1. The paper of the American Association of Colleges for Teacher Education (AACTE) "21st century skills and educator preparation". *Materials website partnership for 21st century skills.* Online access: http://www.p21.org/storage/documents/aacte_p21_whitepaper

2. Ankudinov, A. B., & Lebedev, O. V. (2013). Empirical analysis of employees with tertiary education occupational imbalances. *American Journal of Applied Sciences, 10*(10), 1134–1139. doi:10.3844/ajassp.2013.1134.1139. ISSN: 1546–9239 ©2013 Science Publication. Published Online http://www.thescipub.com/ajas.toc

3. Professional Standard "Management (Leadership) Organization". *Materials website ConsultantPlus.* Online access: http://www.consultant.ru/sys/

4. Grudtcyna, L. I. U. Economic mechanisms of management higher educational institutions. *Education and law -The Official Publication of the Financial University the Government of the Russian Federation, 8*(24). ISSN-2076-1503. Online access: http://education.law-books.ru/eng/index.php?page=upravlenie-obrazovaniem

5. Official website of university *Mari State University.* Online access: http://marsu.ru/structur/BasicUnits/institute/iuif/

6. Savostyanova, I. L. (2013). The problems of availability and relevance of information competence in the professional activity of the modern economist. *Modern Problems of Science and Education 5*(2013). ISSN-2070-7428. © 2013 Russian academy of natural history. Published online: http://www.science-education.ru/en/111-10584

7. Official Website of University. *Kazan (Volga Region) Federal University.* Online access: http://kpfu.ru/main_page?p_sub=16

Software Risk Management: Using the Automated Tools

Sergey M. Avdoshin and Elena Y. Pesotskaya

Abstract Software development process nowadays faces many challenges and risks. In order to manage risks we need to understand the scope and objectives of the software developments and use the appropriate automated risk management tool. The study addresses software risk management in software development area and an approach to analysis, structuring, and evaluating risk with the help of specialized automated tools. The author provides recommendations on how to define a set of selection criteria for automated tools and analyses the growing demand for service hosting solutions and web-applications, stressing that almost any software including risk management tools can be successfully run using this method.

Keywords Software risks • Risk management • Risk management software • Risk management tools • Web-based applications • SaaS solution

1 Introduction

There are many risks involved in creating high quality software that need to be carefully managed. Despite new technology, innovative methods and tools, different management methods—development process still full of risks from the beginning to the end. Therefore, to make sure a project successful we require managing specific IT risks related to our software projects: identify risks and store in a shared data storage, assess risks, using specialized tools and techniques, choose appropriate mitigation action and track that mitigated risks are lower when they were. The need for project risk management has been widely recognized by all software development companies such as Microsoft, SAP, Oracle, IBM etc. Being a development companies they usually use their own powerful automated tools to minimize losses and maximize software development success. As the purpose of project risk management is to improve project performance by systematically identifying and assessing risks, developing strategies to reduce or avoid risks, and maximizing

S.M. Avdoshin (✉) • E.Y. Pesotskaya
Software Management Department, School of Software Engineering, National Research University Higher School of Economics, Moscow, Russian Federation
e-mail: savdoshin@hse.ru; Epesotskaya@hse.ru

© Springer International Publishing Switzerland 2016   85
J. Becker et al. (eds.), *Emerging Trends in Information Systems*, Progress in IS,
DOI 10.1007/978-3-319-23929-3_8

opportunities [1], risk management tools should support a continuous risk management process throughout the life cycle of a system. Effective risk management depends on risk management planning; early identification and analyses of risks; early implementation of corrective actions; continuous monitoring and reassessment; communication, documentation, and coordination. The science of risk management was developed back in the sixteenth century during the Renaissance, a period of discovery, but regarding the subject of Risk Management Process (RMP), since 1990 a large number of methodologies and methods have been generated to address the need for more effective risk management [2]. Among them we can distinguish the PUMA [3] and the MRMP [4] in construction engineering context; the RFRM [5] in system engineering context; the SHAMPU [1] and the PMBoK [6] in project management context; the standard of the AS/NZS 4360 [7] and the DoD [8] in public application context, etc. In the present paper, we have investigated and compared most of risk related topics in software engineering context and automated tools that support risk management process.

Risk management should begin at the earliest stages of program planning and continue throughout the total life-cycle of the program. Additionally, risk management is most effective if it is supported with automated tool that ensures integration with the program's systems engineering and program management processes.

Common practices, concerning risk management is to identify and track issues and risks and then manage the root causes or the consequences (if we were not successful while managing root causes). But also the objective of a proper risk management tools is to provide a repeatable process for balancing cost, schedule, and performance goals within program funding, especially on programs with designs that approach or exceed the state-of-the-art or have tightly constrained or optimistic cost, schedule, and performance goals. Successful risk management depends on the knowledge gleaned from assessments of all aspects of the program coupled with appropriate mitigations applied to the specific root causes and consequences.

Software risk management is not a stand-alone task. It is supported by a number of other tasks as the results of risk management are used to finalize requirements development, logical solution, systems engineering, cost estimating, schedule development, performance measurement, etc.

1.1 Process and Tools for Software Risk Management

In software development process risk management concerns all aspects of the program life cycle phases as they relate to each other, from initiation to disposal. There are basic risks that are generic to almost all software projects. In reality many IT projects are very similar at a high, strategic level. They differ in people involved and exact events. An effective risk management process requires a commitment on the part of the project manager, the project team, and the contractor to be successful.

The project team and management should establish a risk management process that includes not only risk planning, but also risk identification, risk analysis, risk mitigation planning, risk mitigation plan implementation, and risk tracking to be integrated and continuously applied throughout the whole program. For that purposed some automated risk management tools provide seamless integration with Microsoft® Project to quantify the cost and schedule uncertainty associated with project plans. Other tools have possibilities of integration with Microsoft® Excel and illustrate many possible outcomes, e.g. cost and schedule histograms in your Microsoft® Excel spreadsheet.

In the planning phase, the goal of successful risk management is to adapt risk management to the organization's existing project and risk management practices and to document the resulting processes in a risk management plan. Any computerized tools, databases or forms are installed. Project personnel is being trained both in the processes to be carried out and in the methods and tools to use. Finally, the risk management activities must be started and become habitual routine within the project.

Also before we start the software risk management, several questions should be answered:

- What do we expect from risk management?
- Who would participate, how often?
- What skills, competencies are required for risk management?
- What are the main risk management steps and deliverables?
- What actions would be conducted on each step?
- What instruments and methods should be applied at each step?
- What terminology do we use?
- What are the criteria for risk prioritization?
- What response actions should be taken for risk avoidance, mitigation?
- How we should monitor the risk response actions?
- What control activities we apply to the risk management process?
- How often we do reporting on risk management?
- What supporting tools do we use (database, software tools, metafiles, communication channels, etc.)

The automated tool selected for risk management purposes should be integrated with the risk management process methodology and involve five basic steps [1, 6]:

1. Identify the risks—Understand the typical problems that might adversely affect the project.
2. Assess the risks—Rank the risks in order of importance based on probability of occurrence, impact of occurrence, and degree of risk certainty.
3. Plan the risk response—Analyze risk assessment alternatives and modify the project plan to adjust for the risk.
4. Monitor the risks—Throughout the project, continue to revisit the risk profile, re-evaluate major risks, and update the risk profile with action taken.

#	(1)	(2)	(3)	(4)	(5)	(6)	(7)	(8)
	Risk name	Description	Category	Root cause	Consequence	Triggers	Risk owner	Status

Fig. 1 Risk register sample

5. Document lessons learned—Learn from the risk identification, assessment, and management process.

During the first step in the software risk management process, risks should be identified by the project team and interested parties and added to the list of known risks. The automated tool usually supports many techniques for identifying risks, including interviewing questionnaires, reporting, decomposition, assumption analysis, critical path analysis, SWOT, etc. Identifying software risks involves collecting information about the software development project and classifying it to determine the amount of potential risk to the project. Identification procedures include as many participants as possible: team members, experts, functional departments, sponsor, end users, other interested parties. It does not mean all the interested parties need the access to the risk management tool. It depend on the risk management process organization how the information would get to the system. As an output for risk identification stage—risk register should appear (Fig. 1 shows an example).

Sometimes Risk Register contains some extended fields that should be filled in the later stages of risk management, e.g.:

- Risk responsible—person who will take responsibility for each risk (might be the same as risk owner);
- A rank for risk as a result of risk prioritization;
- Potential responses to each risk;
- The probability and impact of each risk occurring.

The successful Project Manager should lead a discussion amongst the team and sponsors to determine the high, medium, and low categories based on the Risk Scores, and assign responses to those categories.

The value of software tool is increased if there are software checklists available. Some tools have predefined risk categories as not all identified risks should be treated the same. Some identified risks are more likely to occur, and some, if realized, would have a bigger impact. Risk analysis and management depends on the types of risks being considered.

Within the context of the technological and business perspectives, there can be distinguished different categories of software risk, for example:

- *Technical risks* that associated with the performance of the software product and include problems with languages, project size, project functionality, platforms, methods, quality, reliability and timeliness issues. Even if there are no mid-project changes in scope, unforeseen technical complications can also turn the project upside down. Project managers might know the technologies they are using in the project very well but still surprises are possible—this component has always been working fine but now when you integrate it with another component, it's a complete mess. The more experienced the technical people are, the lower the risk of unforeseen technical limitations is, but still this risk is always present [9].

- *Standards*, or processes risks may result from excessive constraints, lack of experience, lack of management experience and training, communication problems, organizational issues, lack of authority, and control problems.
- *Financial risks* include cash flow, capital and budgetary issues, and return on investment constraints. These risks are associated with the cost of the software product during software development, including its final delivery, which includes the following issues: budget, nonrecurring costs, recurring costs, fixed costs, variable costs, profit/loss margin, and realism.
- *Personnel risks* include staffing lags, experience and training problems, ethical and moral issues, staff conflicts, and productivity issues. Other resource risks include unavailability or late delivery of equipment & supplies, inadequate tools, inadequate facilities, distributed locations, unavailability of computer resources, and slow response times.
- *Schedule and scope risks* are associated with the schedule and scope of the software product during development. Changes in scope are frequent in IT projects and to some extent they are quite logical—no matter how detailed your specification is, there are always suggestions that come after you have started the implementation.

Often these suggestions demand radical changes and require change requests that can turn any schedule upside down. In order to address the holistic view of risks, software manager should view the risks from a different viewpoint and then get complete information. Also the scope can be affected by technical complications. If a given functionality can't be implemented because it is technically impossible, the easiest solution is to skip this functionality but when other components depend on it, doing this isn't wise.

Risk identification and risk assessment should be done as early as possible to minimize negative deviations and to maximize positive results during project development. Assessing software risks means determining the effects of potential risks. For the purposes of risk assessment the automated tool might provide predefined set of criteria that would help the experts to conduct evaluation. Risks should be assessed by two dimensions—probability and impact. The project team will take these two dimensions and multiply them together to generate a risk score, so the risks can easily be ranked and ordered, allowing for the team and sponsors to dialog about how to respond to each risk. The Risk Score helps us determine a sense of priority amongst the risks. If, for example, the first risk has a score of $100 K and the second of $160 K, then the second risk represents a bigger threat to the project's baselines and has bigger priority.

Fig. 2 Risk severity matrix

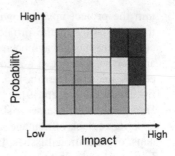

For each risk assessment, the project team must establish how the actual assessment (root cause identification and risk analysis) will be conducted. Having teams outside the project team may be appropriate if the resources needed to do the assessment are beyond those available from within the program team. This team is the core group of individuals who will conduct the risk assessment and normally includes individuals with expertise in systems engineering, logistics, manufacturing, testing, schedule analysis, and cost estimating.

The most widely used technique, that supported by almost all risk management tools is called "Risk map" or "Risk severity matrix" that assess risk probability/likelihood and impact of the potential risk (Fig. 2).

The zone with highest probability and impact (in the upper right corner) identifies the most important events, medium zone lists risks that are moderately important and the lower zone events probably can be safely ignored. Project manager might tune the automated tool to customize which combinations of probability and impact result in a risk's being classified as high risk, moderate risk, and low risk.

For the extended quantitative analysis you might need more complex tool functionality, such as:

- Monte Carlo simulation;
- Sensitivity and Scenario analysis;
- Sensitivity analysis;
- Probabilistic branching;
- Tornado charts and scatter plots;
- Conditional "If-Then-Else" capability;
- Risk histograms;
- Six sigma functions, etc.

The team members assess (identify and analyze) risks and their root causes using documented risk assessment criteria. An ongoing/continual risk assessment is highly recommended, and is useful during all phases of a program's life cycle. A tailored program risk assessment should be conducted for each of the applicable technical reviews and for each key program decision point. Also project team members report and recommend appropriate risk mitigation strategies for each identified root cause, and estimate funding requirements to implement risk mitigation plans with further documentation and knowledge sharing.

The activity of mitigating and avoiding software risks is based on information gained from the previous activities of identifying, planning, and assessing risks. Usually the predefined mitigation action categories, such as avoidance, minimization, transference, limitation, etc. are available. The types of responses can vary depending on the chosen methodology, but the main four types of responses are:

1. Mitigate the Risk—incorporate specific plans into the project scope to deal with the occurrence of, or to minimize the likelihood of, the risk occurring;
2. Avoid the Risk—remove scope that includes risk from the project;
3. Share the Risk—transfer ownership of scope to another party so they now have risk;
4. Accept the Risk—do nothing, run the chance of the risk occurring, deal with it if it does.

Risk reporting is based on information obtained from the previous topics and compares risk status against previously identified risks. Risk reporting provides capabilities to visualize risk information in graphs and charts that can be further exported to Excel, Word, and PowerPoint in native chart format for easy distribution to others.

Risk monitoring and documentation of lessons learned finalize the risk management processes. Usage of the risk database from past projects to plan current projects can help the managers to avoid most already known problems and lets them learn not from their own mistakes, but employ best practice experience and project expertise.

The final phase, improve and expand, starts when basic risk management practices have been implemented in the project. Improvement is needed to ensure that risk management is more and more integrated into normal project risk management and to make the processes, methods and tools more effective. Lessons learned should be documented. Also continuous training and facilitation is required. Risk management should also be expanded to other projects within the organization.

Effective risk management requires involvement of the entire program team and may also require help from outside experts knowledgeable in critical risk areas such as threat, technology, design, manufacturing, logistics, schedule, cost, etc. Overall the extended project team carries out risk management and mitigation activities. Risk management is the responsibility of the Project Manager. However, all project stakeholders should participate in the risk identification and analysis process.

External experts may include representatives from the user, laboratory, contract management, specialty engineering, test and evaluation, logistics and industry. End product users, being essential participants in program trade analyses, should be part of the assessment process so that an acceptable balance among performance, schedule, cost, and risk can be reached. A close relationship between the project team and industry, and later with the selected contractor(s), promotes an understanding of program risks and assists in developing and executing the management efforts.

1.2   How to Select an Automated Risk Management Tool

In order to offer high-quality software products to the market on time and as per the market's requirements, it is important to find computer-based tools with high accuracy probability to help managers make their decision. Software risk analysis and management can be partially transferred into data analysis or data mining. Automated tools are designed to assist project managers in planning and setting up projects, assigning resources to tasks, tracking progress, managing budgets, requirements, changes and risks as well as analyzing workloads.

What should be the selection criteria for an automated tool? It depends on the purpose of risk management in the given software development project and the needs of the team members.

Risk analysis and management are usually based on the information collected from traditional knowledge, or similar well-known cases, common sense, results of experiments or tests, reviewing of inadvertent exposure. The first thing for the automated tools is to collect historical data to build up a database. Once the database exists, it will process the data and mine some useful information to help the manager analyze risks and make decisions. Today's tools can automatically store all project results in a central repository shared by all users. Requirements and changes can be edited, specified and prioritized. Tasks are derived from requirements, which can be traceable through the entire life cycle. This means that *data storage and analysis* should be an important criterion when choosing the system.

Specified risk management software sometimes contains features for test management and quality assurance of the project. Special views and individual reports help project managers assign resources to tasks even in a multi-project environment. Integration with existing testing, quality, cost, and schedule applications might be essential for identification of related testing, quality, cost, and schedule risks. In this case we need to check if the tool has *integration or compatibility with specific applications*.

Most of risk management software supports core risk methodologies, such as CMMI, SPICE, PRINCE2, COBiT etc. For example, the Software Tools Complex for Evaluation of Information Systems Operation Quality (CEISOQ) is designed in accordance with the ISO/IEC 15288 standard and is used to evaluate probabilities of "success", cost, time and quality risks and related profitability and expenses. *Supporting guidance and standards* might be the other important criteria for system selection.

Supporting guidance, standards. and risk methodologies would help users solve on the scientific basis the following practical issues in the system life cycle: analysis of quality management systems for enterprises, substantiation of quantitative system requirements to hardware, software, users, staff, technologies; requirements analysis, the evaluation of project engineering decisions; investigation of problems concerning potential threats to system operation including information security and protection against terrorists; evaluation of system operation quality, substantiation of recommendations for rational system use and optimization etc. [10].

There are lots of methods in Machine Learning study. For example, clustering skills are used to assign risk label to different risks. In each cluster, risks may have similar attributes. Association rule method is used to analyze each cluster to find the relationship between risks and risks factors. Some other artificial intelligence methods (9 K-near neighbor approach, ID3 decision tree, Neuro-Network, etc) are used to build risk assessment models and to predict risks of software development. *Supporting specific functionality* might also be a criterion when choosing a tool.

Sometimes, in environments where risk assessments are performed but are not standardized, risk evaluations may vary from one assessor to the next. Whether an appropriate action is taken depends on the particular assessor, meaning that similar issues may end up being treated differently. To avoid inconsistent risk assessments a single system should be used to collect and manage risk management related activities. The system should guarantee that corporate risk tolerance thresholds are employed and followed for risk-related activities across the whole IT project. Thus, we can define important criteria of *standardized risk calculation tools and methodologies*.

In the market, there are all kinds of popular software for decision making that is also applicable for risk management in software risks analysis even if with certain limitation. Microsoft SQL Server, Crystal Decisions, Microsoft OLAP/Analysis Services are successful decision making software used in business domain. As software development risks can be viewed from different perspectives, even though different from banking, trading business, it does a kind of a hybrid business.

Different criteria may be used while selecting an appropriate risk management tools, such as:

- Data storage/centralized repository and data analysis engines?
- Check lists for software risks?
- Risk assessment capabilities?
- Integration points? (e.g. Microsoft Project/Excel integration)
- Use of graphs and charts?
- Monte-Carlo simulation (other critical functionality)?
- Customizable features?
- Web-based?
- Compatibility?
- Reporting techniques?
- Supporting guidance and standards, etc.

Among specialized risk management software the most popular are: Risk+, Risk Radar®, Risk Watch, IBM Rational Portfolio Manager, OCTAVE-S, CRAMM, Citicus ONE, SCIENTECH, @Risk, ClearRisk, Primavera Risk Analysis, Active Risk Manager, withRISK, Protecht.ERM, Risk Wizard, etc.

There might arise on obvious question: does it make sense to buy off-the-shelf, packaged applications or it is cheaper to create custom solutions (built in-house or with outsourced developers)? To make the decision, several factors should be considered between build and buy. We should analyze technical capabilities, time to market, functionality, support ability, conduct financial analysis and calculate return on investment. Of course, packaged software has many benefits: it is available for many common information technology needs, tested and proved. Most of the packages today come with the global best practices, future upgrades and support, but they not always show a perfect fit with business needs. That's why it is also reasonable to understand the degree of compliance of tools with traditional business processes and rules.

1.3 Tools Evolution

Today we have a great choice of different technologies and may use software as we need. Many software users prefer computer tools with much lower setup time. They want to forget about installation, implementation, training and maintenance efforts.

Today, the value is not defined as much by functionality anymore but by connectivity. The user seems to move from process focus and client server architecture to distributed functions and data centric software with real-time connectivity. As business applications continue to mature, a number of new technology and technology adoption discontinuities (social, cloud and mobile) are providing opportunities for users and vendors alike.

While interest in cloud technology and cloud economics abounds, Forrester [11] believes that cloud computing's greatest benefits will come from changes to the IT technology and organizational model. IT decision makers expect the external cloud to play a major role in hosting selected application workloads in the near future. Having the choice between enterprise solutions and web solutions, risk managers might decide on appropriate functional option and price.

As IT project is usually a temporary initiative with defined beginning and end dates, sometimes it makes sense not to purchase a standalone automated software tool for the purpose of risk management, but to get an instant web access to all required functionality, such as identifying, analyzing, tracking, mitigating, and controlling project risks. Choosing web-based or mobile solution customers do not pay for owning the software itself but rather for using it.

Where customers may have little interest or capability in software deployment, but do have substantial computing needs, hosting services (SaaS—Software as a Service) is an attractive option. Activities that are managed from central locations rather than at each customer's site, enabling team members to access applications remotely via the *Web*. It allows risk management team to concentrate on their day-to-day software development activities, rather than conducting risk management tool support, administration, security monitoring, new techniques implementation and training.

Web application service hosting allows decreasing large upfront costs as it usually provides free trials, also contains no install costs (only one-time costs) and includes operating costs only.

The lesson of cloud computing is that relatively cheap hardware using virtualization and embedded functionality brings flexibility in computing, storage and network capacity, and management, and enormous improvements in administration.

The main advantages of web-based risk management tools are quick and easy installation and setup and intuitive user-oriented design, when the user can start entering and managing the risks in a very little time. System access via a secure internet/intranet connection makes deployment quick, convenient and easy.

The functionality of such systems usually supports the main risk operations, such as categorizing, prioritizing, modeling, tracking and reporting identified risks. Global availability, access to the software from any machine, cost saving (as there are no hardware costs) and lack of IT support make web-serviced risk management solutions more and more popular. Of course, such services have disadvantages, such as low customization possibilities, work with predefined functionality where managing and tracking functional changes is a challenge, difficulties with other applications integration. This explains the fact, that many risk management software providers have a range of software solutions—from "heavy" client/server application with risk check lists and extensive range of risk management capabilities currently available to "light" web solutions that enable easier and cheaper access to the core risk management functionality. This does not mean that a single web-based tool for managing risks and opportunities cannot be used to meet all the needs of different IT stakeholders and team members. It depends on the risk management purpose and the scale of risk management activities and parties involved, so a customer may choose exactly the solution he or she needs.

Software development projects can be compared to small enterprises, which are normally early adopters of hosting-services solutions because:

- They can't afford to purchase the costly in-house developed/packaged solutions
- They do not have time and effort for support and maintenance an auxiliary IT solution
- They enjoy easy web-access and access from mobile devices at any time
- The cloud technology is good enough to meet the needs of a small team

After an IT development project is over and there is no need to manage IT risks, the IT project team can easily unsubscribe from the risk management services after paying all rental license fees for the application to the service provider.

2 Summary

Today we have a great choice of different technologies and may use software as we need. Many software users prefer computer tools with much lower setup time. They want to forget about installation, implementation, training and maintenance efforts.

It is a common opinion that an IT project is always over budget, behind schedule and unreliable. Usage of additional automated tools for risk management purposes sometimes seems useless and costly and project teams face the possibility of losing critical risks, poor communication of risks issues between the interested parties, lack of interest from senior executives due to inability of proper analysis and reporting. This happens because software development and implementation is a complicated process which involves many concerned parties with different expectations. A typical IT project has many interdependent components and modifications, and delays in one component can easily affect everything else. An automated risk management tool does not guarantee success, but serves the primary goal of storage and analysis of identified issues, timely responding with sufficient lead time to avoid crises, involvement of all interested parties into the risk management process, so that it becomes possible to carry out a project that meets its target and provide users and managers with greater confidence in IT. The proposed risk management tools and methods help project managers deal with risk management programs in a most effective and efficient manner.

It is clear that each software project is unique and needs adaptation and customization of selected automated tools to its practical implementation. In this article the author recommends to define a set of selection criteria for automated tools. This set of criteria should be defined for each specific IT project and consider the goals of implementation, objectives of risk management process, the size of IT team and their needs, the possibility of integration with required standards and methodologies, necessity of web access, integration possibilities with Office applications, etc.

Also we should consider the growing demand for service hosting solutions and web-applications which are licensed for use as a service and provided to customers on demand. Cloud technologies become increasingly popular in software deployment as companies prefer to run software on a vendor's or service provider's server with payment based on subscription or time used instead of an individual license. Using web services users interact with the software via a portal on their laptops or mobile devices, almost any software including risk management tools can be run using this method and show good results.

References

1. Chapman, C. B., & Ward, S. C. (2003). *Project risk management, processes, techniques and insights* (2nd ed.). Chichester: Wiley.
2. Kwak, Y. A., & Stoddard, J. (2003). Project risk management: Lessons learned from software development environment. *Technovation, 24*, 915–920.

3. Del Cano, A., & De La Cruz, M. P. (2002). Integrated methodology for project risk management. *Journal of Construction Engineering and Management, 128*(6), 473–485.
4. Pipattanapiwong, J. (2004). *Development of multi-party risk and uncertainty management process for an infrastructure project.* PhD thesis, Kochi University of Technology. Kochi, Japan.
5. Haimes, Y. Y., Kaplan, S., & Lambert, J. H. (2002). Risk filtering, ranking and management framework using hierarchical holographic modeling. *Risk Analysis, 22*(2), 381–395.
6. PMI (Project Management Institute). (2004). *A guide to the project management body of knowledge (PMBoK).* Newtown Square. Pennsylvania.
7. Cooper, D. *Tutorial notes: The Australian and New Zealand standard on risk management (AS/NZS 460).* Retrieved from May, 2004 http://www.broadleaf.com
8. Conrow, E. H. (2003). *Effective risk management: Some keys to success* (2nd ed.). Reston, VA: American Institute of Aeronautics and Astronautics.
9. Lian, X. *Software project management – Risk management (Abstraction).* http://www.docstoc.com/docs/24840578/Software-Project-Management
10. Avdoshin, S., & Pesotskaya, E. (2011). *Business informatization. Managing risks.* Moscow: DMK Press. 176 p. [in Russian].
11. Garbani, J.-P., Cecere, M. (2011, May 3). *IT infrastructure and operations: The next five years.* Cambridge: Forrester Research.

Integrating Case Studies into Information Security Education

Alexandra Savelieva and Sergey Avdoshin

Abstract Today the demand is growing for information security experts capable of analyzing problems and making decisions in business situations that involve risk or uncertainty. These skills can be acquired through systematic studying of various information security incidents. In this paper we propose a framework of methods, tools and taxonomies for analysis of case studies in information security field. Our framework allows to study every situation in a formal rather than ad-hoc way, and apply a wide range of threat modeling, risk analysis and project management techniques under lifelike conditions. We illustrate it by providing two case studies based on real situations: a conflict between a free email service provider and a commercial bank, and an attack on a famous security company by a powerful hacktivist group. The first situation explores the risks of using cloud services, while the second highlights the importance of applying secure code principles for in-house software development. Although the cases are seemingly different, we demonstrate that they can be analyzed with similar tools.

Keywords Case study • Information security • Education • Security incident • Event chain • Parkerian Hexad • Threat • STRIDE • Information asset • Risk • Attack lifecycle

1 Introduction

One of inherent skills in information systems engineering and support is the ability to ensure appropriate level of information security. Information security and privacy have become core concepts in information system education [1]. However, related disciplines at colleges and universities tend to be limited to technical and

This work was done in 2011–2012 when Alexandra Savelieva was with Higher School of Economics in Moscow, Russia. Now she is working in Microsoft Corporation in Redmond, USA.

A. Savelieva
Microsoft Corporation, Redmond, WA, USA

S. Avdoshin (✉)
National Research University Higher School of Economics, Moscow, Russia
e-mail: savdoshin@hse.ru

© Springer International Publishing Switzerland 2016
J. Becker et al. (eds.), *Emerging Trends in Information Systems*, Progress in IS,
DOI 10.1007/978-3-319-23929-3_9

mathematical principles of information protection, leaving human factor and risk management aspects outside of the scope. This gap between business requirements and existing educational practices in the field is currently attracting a lot of attention worldwide, and the case study method is rapidly gaining popularity as a teaching tool that has already proved useful in a wide range of areas where specialists need to make decisions in the situations that involve risk or uncertainty.

Case studies are stories with educational message [2]. Case study method was introduced in the beginning of twentieth century in Harvard Business School primarily for development of analytical and problem-solving skills among training lawyers and managers.

Currently educational institutions in the US are actively working on adopting case study method into the educational practice of teaching information security and assurance. National Science Foundation sponsored a project titled "Developing Case Studies for Information Security Curriculum" (2008–2011). In May 2012 three US universities, North Carolina A&T State University, the University of North Carolina at Charlotte, and the University of Tennessee at Chattanooga, have collaboratively conducted a Workshop on Teaching Information Assurance through Case Studies and Hands-on Experiences [3]. The purpose of the workshop is to provide concrete case studies, and hands-on lab material, test questions, and evaluation rubrics that can be applied in teaching information assurance (IA) in computing related courses. Participants with diverse backgrounds were encouraged to participate and share innovative IA teaching techniques that could be later adopted by multiple disciplines such as computer science, software engineering, information technology, and business. Case study analysis was enlisted in Ref. [4] among the skills that students at both undergraduate and graduate levels should embrace as a security professional.

In Europe, the importance of engaging information security students in 'active learning' is also recognized. For example, a team from the University of Twente (Netherlands) have recently published the results of their experiment of introducing a new course entitled "Cyber Crime Science", which focuses on the social aspects of thinking thief [5]. Instead of taking the usual point of view of the security engineer, the professors challenged their master students to take the point of view of a motivated offender. The crime science experiment technique adopted in the course inspired the students for doing deep self-paced research, motivating the team to advocate its place in the curriculum and continue the work in this area.

2 Problem Statement

Major problems that an educator faces when using case studies for teaching practical information security in higher school are as follows [6]:

- Lack of ready-made materials are available for free use, apart from "product success story" case studies presented on web sites of a few companies for advertisement purposes

- Lack of guidelines for using case studies in information security classroom and integrating the method into the academic curriculum

In Ref. [7], we have shown how to build a fascinating and relevant story from scratch without much efforts from the teacher, but with high benefit to the audience. Our educational materials at the moment include guidelines for writing new case studies in information security, and a permanently growing library which currently consists of 30+ case studies in Russian and English. In Ref. [8], authors come up with an alternative solution of using scenarios drawn from political science, history, and other humanities to force students to apply or derive principles of computer security to unusual and unexpected situations.

The second problem has not been studied yet, although the importance of guidelines for using case studies is widely recognized (as stated in Ref. [9], 95 % of the most popular cases have teaching notes). Educational centers that charge organizations for the use of their materials (e.g. European Case Clearing House and Harvard Business for Educators) typically supplement their case studies with a section of comments and/or expert opinions (see e.g. Ref. [10]), in order to facilitate the class discussion and help the teacher identify and address key issues in the case. Such guidelines are very instrumental, but their use is limited to the concrete case.

Purpose of our work. In this paper, we focus on designing a framework for case study analysis specific to the information security field. In contrast to existing work where teaching notes are provided on case-by-case basis, we aim at providing a unified set of tools that would allow the educator to get to the root problems of any case study. For this purpose, we bring together methods from project management, threat modeling, and risk analysis. We apply our framework to real stories in order to demonstrate that our approach allows to deal with different situation in a common way and helps students acquire important skills and activate theoretical knowledge. We justify integrate case study method in information security curriculum of B.Sc. and M.Sc. students at Higher School of Economics, and share the results of our experience.

3 Framework Components and Applications

The majority of case studies for information security classes are based on a situation made up of one or more unwanted or unexpected events that have compromised, or could very likely compromise, the security of an information asset and affect the business operations. Authors of [4] argue that planning for and managing failure must be explicitly taught as a part of the post-incident process, to assure that students are capable of strengthening an organization's information security.

The most important concepts for case study analysis are, therefore, *information security event* and *information security incident*. According to the standard ISO/IEC 27001:2005 [11], information security event is *"an identified occurrence of a system, service or network state indicating a possible breach of information security policy or failure of safeguards, or a previously unknown situation that may be security relevant*", and information security incident is "*a single or a series of unwanted or unexpected information security events that have a significant probability of compromising business operations and threatening information security*". These definitions are used as a starting point for our framework. We use a bottom-up approach to redefine the concepts so that they become instrumental for case study analysis, i.e. we start with the formulation of a few basic definitions in Sect. 3.1, then we use them as building blocks for more complicated concepts of information security event (Sect. 3.2), and, finally, information security incident (Sect. 3.3). Guidelines for application of the framework to case studies are presented in Sect. 3.4, with an example provided in Sect. 3.5.

3.1 Elements of Case Study: Terminology and Relationships

In this section we introduce terms and definitions that are used in the rest of the paper, and link our ideas to the existing body of knowledge in information security.

Definition 1 Information security risk *refers to probability and impact of an information security property violation threat.*

Definition 2 Information security property *is a subset of six fundamental elements of information security (Confidentiality, Possession or control, Integrity, Authenticity, Availability, and Utility)* [12, 13] *that can be attributed to an information asset.*

Definition 3 Information asset *is a piece of information that is valuable to an organization.*

Definition 4 Threat *is a process that can lead to violation of information security property.*

Definition 5 Malicious activity *refers to behavior of a person or a system that produces one or more threats.*

3.2 Case Study Analysis: Static Perspective

Conceptual schema of information security event can be built based on the elements introduced in Sect. 3.1. Figure 1 shows a map of the concepts, and relations between them. In order to connect Definition 4 to Definition 1, we use threat taxonomy called STRIDE [14] and set up a mapping to the Parkerian Hexad [12, 13].

The advantage of having information security property linked to STRIDE threat model is the availability of mitigation techniques based on threat type. For example recommendations for protection against tampering include Windows Vista

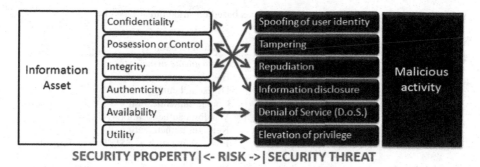

Fig. 1 Conceptual schema of information security event elements

Mandatory Integrity Controls, ACLs, Digital signatures, and Message authentication codes (see Table 1 and Secure Development Lifecycle (SDL) in Ref. [14] for more details). This is particularly useful for students who study software engineering, since they can see the importance of writing secure code on concrete examples, identify pitfalls of information system designers and propose ideas for threat mitigation using techniques and best practices from SDL methodology.

By providing possibility of a simple transition from threat to mitigation strategy, our paper makes a step forward compared to existing publications in this area which serve mainly for descriptive purposes (e.g. computer system attack classifications and taxonomies suggested in Ref. [15–18], or the paper proposing common language for computer security incidents [19]).

3.3 Case Study Analysis: Dynamic Perspective

The formalization from Sect. 3.2 is limited in terms of taking a static snapshot of the situation. When data within an information system get compromised, this is typically a result of a series of events, including several steps of attacks launched by the adversary. Moreover, each step of an attack often depends on the previous step being successful. One of existing representations of an attack lifecycle depicted in Fig. 2 differentiates between the following attack stages (see [20]):

– Reconnaissance—the adversary collects data to plan further actions
– Penetration—the adversary gets unauthorized access to the information system component(s)
– Information damage—the adversary performs actions that affect security properties of information assets within the target system
– Proliferation—the adversary prepares for further intrusions by taking the advantage of the achieved results

As pointed in Ref. [4], one of the important activities in a case exercise is how to create a timeline that should allow students to visually insert players at some point

Table 1 Mitigation techniques and technologies based on stride threat type [14]

Threat type	Mitigation technique	Mitigation technology
Spoofing	Authentication	*To authenticate principals:* Basic authentication Digest authentication Cookie authentication Windows authentication (NTLM) Kerberos authentication PKI systems such as SSL/TLS and certificates IPSec Digitally signed packets *To authenticate code or data:* Digital signatures Message authentication codes Hashes
Tampering	Integrity	Windows Vista Mandatory Integrity Controls ACLs Digital signatures Message Authentication Codes
Repudiation	Non-repudiation	Strong Authentication Secure logging and auditing Digital Signatures Secure time stamps Trusted third parties
Information Disclosure	Confidentiality	Encryption ACLs
Denial of Service	Availability	ACLs Filtering Quotas Authorization High availability designs
Elevation of Privilege	Authorization	ACLs Group or role membership Privilege ownership Permissions Input validation

of time, and to see the impacts on the incident and response. In order to incorporate the dynamic nature of information security incidents into our case study analysis framework, we propose to use a simplified version of a visualization technique referred to as Event Chain Diagram [21]. Such diagrams show the relationships between events and how the events affect each other. By using this technique which originates from project management, we can simplify the analysis of information security risks and represent the flow of events in a visual form (see Fig. 3). Each square corresponds to an event which had, or could have, some impact on information security property of one or more assets.

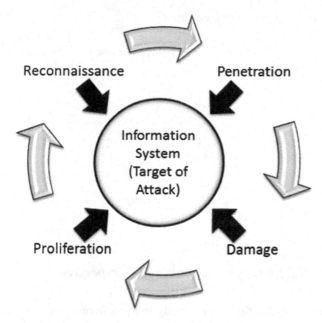

Fig. 2 Lifecycle of attack [20]

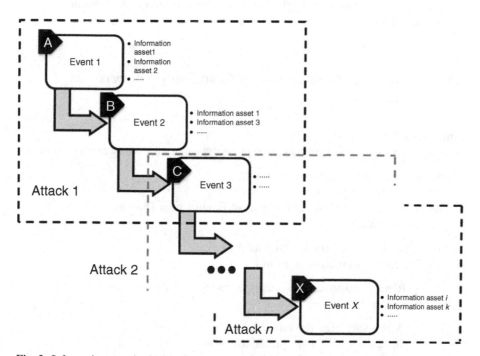

Fig. 3 Information security incident as an event chain

Table 2 Case study analysis table representation

Event	Asset	Property	Risk		Mitigation	
			Probability	Impact	Precaution	Recovery
A	Inf. asset 1	...	...	...	...	...
	Inf. asset 2	...	...	...	...	
	...	...	...	...	...	
B	Inf. asset 1	...	...	...	...	
	Inf. asset 3	...	...	...	...	
	...	...	...	...	...	
C	...	...	...	...	...	
...	...	...	...	...	...	
X	Inf. asset i	...	...	...	...	
	Inf. asset k	...	...	...	...	
	...	...	...	...	...	

3.4 Case Study Analysis: Combined Perspective

The algorithm for application of case study analysis framework is presented below. Step 4(b)iiA is performed with the help of [12, 13] and mapping shown in Fig. 1. For 4(b)iiC, threat type based mitigations provided in Table 1 (see [14] for details) are instrumental. Results of further analysis are convenient to present in table format (see Table 2).

3.5 Algorithm for Application of Case Study Analysis Framework

Input: Case Study
Output: Event chain diagram; Table representation of case study analysis results

1. Identify information security events E
2. Sort E in chronological order
3. Depict the flow of events E by means of Event Chain Diagram
4. For each event in E

   (a) Identify affected information assets I
   (b) For each information asset in I

      i. Identify information security property violation threats T
      ii. For each threat in T

         A. Specify affected information security property
         B. Evaluate the risk (probability and impact)
         C. Propose methods and best practices for risk mitigation

5. Populate the Table 2

3.6 Applications

We illustrate the application of our case study analysis framework on examples of stories that triggered a lot of discussions in the professional community due to its complicated nature: a conflict between a free email service provider and a commercial bank [22], and an attack on a famous security company by a powerful hacktivist group [23]. The first situation is related to the risks of using cloud services, while the second highlights the importance of applying secure code principles for in-house software development. By applying our framework to the two stories, we demonstrate the versatility of the toolset for case study analysis proposed in Sect. 3. Results of the framework application to the case studies are provided in Appendices A and B.

For those interested in using case studies and our framework in the classroom, we recommend to consider the following security incidents:

- References [24, 25]—a very insightful story about the dependency of modern society on the digital world and the importance of personal data (PII) protection. The analysis of this incident benefits from the application of Attack Lifecycle concept for building Event Chain.
- Reference [26]—a model situation where the breach of data integrity and availability caused a major security incident, while most of the time confidentiality issues tend to draw public attention.
- Reference [27]—a rare example of enterprise-level security incident (APT) which was reported in public press with sufficient level of details which makes it very instrumental for study purposes.
- Reference [28]—a fascinating story from software industry which shows how design flaws resulted in a critical issue in financial market sector. This is not a typical security incident since it does not involve 'bad guys': breaches of Parkerian Hexad properties are caused by software engineers, interface designers and end users.

4 Discussion and Conclusions

4.1 Our Contributions

We designed an instrumental framework for case study analysis specific to the information security field which includes the following tools:

- Conceptual schema for static analysis of information security event
- Event chain visualization for chronological analysis of information security incident
- Table representation template for the results of case study analysis
- Algorithm for applying the above tools to a case study

Our framework provides a unified way to analyze case studies based on an information security incident together with a concise and clear representation of analysis results in the form of a table and/or a diagram. We combined various techniques from threat modeling (STRIDE), project management (Event Chain Diagrams) and information security risk analysis (Parkerian Hexad), and integrated them into our framework. This is also important that we designed our approach in line with ISO/IEC 27001:2005 which belongs to the family of the most popular standards on information security management.

We expect that presented results will be instrumental for information security educators who use case studies in their classes and need a systematic approach to analyze them.

We also expect that information security experts who deal with incident management will find our framework useful, and adopt the tools and artifacts in their work.

4.2 Results

We presented examples of application of our framework to real world situations. More stories have been tested during practical studies with a few groups of students. Our classroom experience has confirmed that the framework is easy to apply but very instrumental for facilitating the discussion. In general, application of case study method in information security classes proved advantageous in terms of:

- Focusing on practical aspects of information security in the real world
- High level of students interest and involvement proved by substantial increase of students attendance
- Articulating the impact of organizational decisions and corporate culture on information security policy
- Demonstration of risk management principles application in the context of information protection
- Reduction of plagiarism in individual students assignments
- Multifaceted approach to information security from the perspective of end user, technical specialist, architect, financial department, and top management

Additionally, we found case studies useful for conducting end-of-course exams. Every student received an individual assignment in the form of case study to analyze using the knowledge and skills they gained from our course. This approach essentially eliminated the possibility of cheating, and allowed us to evaluate the students' ability to apply the course material to an ad-hoc situation.

Our achievements have been recognized as high potential and supported by grants and awards from Microsoft [29], Kaspersky Lab [30] and the Foundation for Educational Innovations of the HSE [31].

4.3   Future Work

Further formalization in terms of ontology and lattice-based models is a straight-forward next step of the research. In this paper, we intentionally refrained from using mathematical notation for the framework, to make sure that the approach is simple enough to be used in classroom discussions. In the future, we are planning to develop software tools that help both the educator and the students apply the framework to a particular case study.

Our intention is to continue with integration of interactive educational methods in the information security curriculum, including application of case studies for final assessment of students competencies acquired during the course. We are also motivated to adopt cyber exercises, the highly interactive approach to exploring information security challenges which is rapidly gaining popularity worldwide, for the purpose of our classes.

Acknowledgements The present work benefited from the input of reviewers and participants of BIR 2012 Workshop on Teaching Business Informatics Intelligent Educational Systems and E-learning, thanks to Dr. Prof. Oleg Kozyrev, Director of HSE Nizhny Novgorod campus, and other members of the organizing committee, who made it possible for the authors to give a talk in teleconference mode. Alexandra Savelieva wishes to thank Oksana Chernenko, Executive Director of the HSE Foundation for Education Innovations, for her support, encouragement and guidance throughout the development of this educational project. The authors also wish to express their gratitude to Dr. Anatoli Shkred, CEO and Rector at INTUIT. RU, and Dr. Alexander Gavrilov, Academic Lead at Microsoft Russia, whose positive feedback and useful comments encouraged them to continue the work after the publication of the first case study-based electronic course on information security. The authors would like to sincerely thank Dr. Prof. Arun Sood, Co-Director, International Cyber Center, for the opportunity to present the idea of using case studies to a broad audience of professional specific target groups involved in cyber security all around the world participating in "2011 Workshop on Cyber Security and Global Affairs", and Dr. Prof. Vladimir Azarov, Deputy Director of Research at MIEM HSE, for the invitation to MQ&ISM-2012 conference collocated with an intensive course on the ISO 27000 series of standards by CIS Austria.

Appendix: A Case Study #1: The Dangers of Keeping Corporate Mail in a Cloud

The first application of our case study analysis framework is a story that triggered a lot of discussions in the professional community due to its complicated nature and interesting background [22]. Event chain for the case study is depicted in Fig. 4.

When the bank employee receives a call from the client, he has no reliable way to verify the identity of the person calling (i.e. the authenticity property of client's request is questionable). We cannot be confident at this point that the email address communicated during this call as the client agent's address was received by the bank employee correctly, due to possible noise at the phone line and human error when reading and writing texts (especially by hand). Although the probability of such error is low, the impact of sending confidential information to an unintended

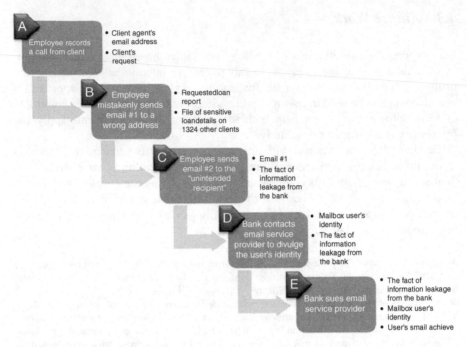

Fig. 4 Case study #1: event chain

recipient is high, as stated in the table for information asset 'Client agent's email address' and security property 'Integrity'.

Next, the employee sends the requested data to the wrong email address. We know that he also attaches a file containing data of 1324 other clients, and that this information should have never left the bank boundaries. Thus, we can assume that neither authorization system to limit the employees' access to sensitive client data nor outgoing mail filtering system were in place. Had it been the case, the utility of this information assets would be zero since the employee would not be able to retrieve it and send to an untrusted address because the email would have been automatically blocked.

Nevertheless, the email did leave the bank. Without evidence that someone read the message, we cannot say that the confidentiality was affected. Instead, the bank lost control of the email information contents (had it been encrypted, there would be no reasons to worry). The bank employee had no way to check whether the email was accessed at all: for example, it could be mistaken by the recipient for spam due to the huge amount of financial fraud spam circulating in the world (as we know from the information about the case revealed later, this was indeed the case: the user put the letter to his junk mail box without even opening it). The information about email status could have been easily retrieved if the email had been sent to a bank corporate mail, or some service rented by the bank from an external mail service provider under appropriate agreement. This was not the case, so the employee followed up with a second email asking the recipient to disregard and remove the previous email and urgently contact the bank for further information. By doing so, he was arguably increasing the probability of the situation when the fact of information leakage from the bank becomes public: even if the user disposed of the previous email, he could become curious about the situation; if not, there was no guarantee that he wouldn't copy the email contents before disposing of the email as requested. In any case, he was very unlikely to contact the bank for clarification.

Further development of the situation affects the email service provider not willing to disclose the recipient's identity due to its user policy without appropriate court order. The Bank then sued the email service provider requesting the user's identity to be revealed and account suspended, insisting that the case should be filed under seal. The information assets and security properties affected at this point were the e-mailbox owner's identity (confidentiality), his or her email archive (availability). Finally, the fact of information leakage from the bank eventually became publicly known.

Table representation of the case study analysis is provided in Table 3.

Table 3 Case study #1 analysis: table representation

Event	Asset	Property	Risk		Mitigation	
			Probability	Impact	Precaution	Recovery
A	Client's request	Authenticity	Medium	Medium	Digital signature, authentication	–
	Client agent's email address	Integrity	Low	High	Security policy	Filtering
B	Requested loan report	Utility	High	Low	Authorization	Filtering
	File of sensitive loan details on 1324 clients	Utility	High	Low	Authorization	Filtering
C	Email contents	Control	Medium	High	Encryptions	Trusted third parties
	The fact of information leakage from the bank	Control	Low	High	–	–
D	Mailbox user's identity	Confidentiality	Low	Low	–	–
	User's mail archive	Availability	Low	High	High availability designs	–
	The fact of information leakage from the bank	Confidentiality	Medium	High	–	–
E	Mailbox user's identity	Confidentiality	High	Low	–	–
	User's mail archive	Availability	Medium	High	High availability designs	–
	The fact of information leakage from the bank	Confidentiality	High	High	–	–

Appendix: B Case Study #2: The Shoemaker's Son Always Goes Barefoot

The situation analyzed in this section is an example of so-called advanced persistent threat, or APT. Unlike case study #1 where the information security breach was a result of a series of mishaps, this story is about a hacker group which intentionally targets its persistent efforts at a specific entity. The irony is that the target entity appears to be a famous company that specializes in providing services in information security area. See [23] and other relevant publications in press and online media for more information on the notorious security incident.

The concept of Attack Lifecycle (Fig. 2 in Sect. 3.3) is very instrumental for building the Event Chain diagram. At the first stage, the target information system is the company custom content management system (CMS) from a third party developer.

– Reconnaissance—the hackers analyze CMS vulnerabilities and discover a possibility to apply SQL injection attack;
– Penetration—the hackers apply SQL injection;
– Information damage—the hackers retrieve CMS contents from the database;
– Proliferation—the hackers identify employees' aliases and hashed passwords as useful piece of information for further extension of the attack.

Proliferation phase of the first attack serves as the Reconnaissance phase for the next attacks, where the target information systems are the support machine and the email service provider used by the company. Penetration involves breaking the cryptographic algorithm MD5 used for hashing users' passwords, and so on.

A simplified information security event chain of the case is presented in Fig. 5.

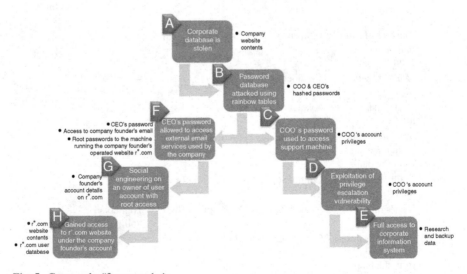

Fig. 5 Case study #2: event chain

Case study analysis table representation is provided below in Table 4. Utility, unlike other security properties, is considered here from the attacker's perspective, i.e. we assume that the information asset is of no utility (useless) to the attacker if handled properly. Therefore, by 'risk' we mean probability and impact of the situation when the information asset becomes useful to the attacker.

Table 4 Case study #2 analysis: table representation

Event	Asset	Property	Risk		Mitigation	
			Probability	Impact	Precaution	Recovery
A	Company website contents	Utility	Low	High	Input validation	Encryption
B	COO & CEO's hashed passwords	Confidentiality	High	High	Security policy	Strong authentication
C	COO's account privileges	Control	High	Low	PKI systems and certificates	Permissions
D	COO's account privileges	Integrity	Low	High	Integrity controls	–
E	Research and backup data	Confidentiality	Medium	High	–	Encryption
	Research and backup data	Availability	Medium	High	High availability designs	–
F	CEO's external email service privileges	Utility	Medium	Low	Security policy	Group or role membership
	Access to the company founder's email	Authenticity	High	Medium	–	–
	Root passwords to the machine running website r*.com	Confidentiality	Medium	Low	Security policy	–
G	Company founder's account details on r*.com	Control	High	High	Digital signatures	Secure logging and auditing
H	r'.com website contents	Integrity	High	High	–	–
	r*.com website user database	Confidentiality	High	High	Encryption	–

References

1. Ayyagari, R., & Tyks, J. (2012). Disaster at a university: A case study in information security. *Journal of Information Technology Education, 11* (Innovations in practice).
2. Herreid, C. F. (Ed.). (2007). *Start with a story: The case study method of teaching science.* Arlington, VA: National Science Teachers Association. pp. 466.
3. Workshop on Teaching Information Assurance Through Case Studies and Hands-on Experiences. http://teaching-ia.appspot.com/
4. Logan, P., & Christofero, T. (2009). Giving failure a place in information security: Teaching students to use the post-mortem as a way to improve security. In: *Proceedings of the 13th colloquium for information systems security education.* University of Alaska, Fairbanks Seattle, WA, June 1–3, 2009.
5. Hartel, P. H., & Junger, M. (2012). *Teaching information security students to "think thief".* Technical report TR-CTIT-12-19, Centre for Telematics and Information Technology, University of Twente, Enschede. ISSN 1381–3625.
6. Savelieva, A. (2011). Special considerations in using the case-study method in teaching information security. In: *Proceedings of "IT security for the next generation".* TUM, Germany: Garching, Boltzmannstr. http://www.kaspersky.com/images/alexandra_savelieva-10-95017.pdf
7. Savelieva, A. A., & Avdoshin, S. M. (2011). Information security education and awareness: Start with a story. In: *Proceedings of "2011 workshop on cyber security and global affairs".* http://www.internationalcybercenter.org/workshops/cs-ga-2011/asavelieva
8. Bishop, M. (2006, September). Teaching context in information security. *Journal on Educational Resources in Computing, 6*(3).
9. Homepage — ECCH for educators. http://www.ecch.com/educators/
10. McNulty, E. (2007). Boss, I think someone stole our customer data. *Harvard Business Review, September,* 37–42.
11. ISO/IEC 27001:2005. (2005). *Information technology security techniques information security management systems requirements.*
12. Parker, D. B. (1998). *Fighting computer crime.* New York: Wiley.
13. Parker, D. B. (2009). Toward a new framework for information security. In S. Bosworth, M. E. Kabay, & E. Whyne (Eds.), *The computer security handbook* (5th ed.). New York: Wiley.
14. Howard, M., & Lipner, S. (2006). *The security development lifecycle: SDL: A process for developing demonstrably more secure software* (pp. 304). Microsoft Press.
15. Landwehr, C. E., & Bull, A. R. (1994). A taxonomy of computer program security flaws, with examples. *ACM Computing Surveys, 26*(3), 211–254.
16. Lindqvist, U., & Jonsson, E. (1997). *How to systematically classify computer security intrusions* (pp. 154–163). IEEE Symposium on Security and Privacy, Los Alamitos, CA.
17. Paulauskas, N., & Garsva, E. (2006). *Computer system attack classification* (2nd ed., Vol. 66). Kaunas: Technology.
18. Weber, D. J. (1998). *A taxonomy of computer intrusions.* Master's thesis, Department of Electrical Engineering and Computer Science, Massachusetts Institute of Technology.
19. Howard, J. D., & Longstaff, T. A. (1998). *A common language for computer security incidents.* Technical report, Sandia National Laboratories.
20. Serdiouk, V. A. (2007). *Advances in technologies for protection against attacks in corporate networks.* Moscow: Tekhnosphera.
21. Event Chain Methodology in Project Management. White Paper by Intaver Institute Inc., http://www.intaver.com/Articles/Article_EventChainMethodology2011.pdf
22. Zetter, K. (2011). *Bank sends sensitive E-mail to wrong Gmail address, Sues Google.* Wired, September 21, 2009. http://www.wired.com/threatlevel/2009/09/bank-sues-google/
23. Bright, P. (2011). *Anonymous speaks: the inside story of the HBGary hack.* ArsTechnica, http://arstechnica.com/tech-policy/news/2011/02/anonymous-speaks-the-inside-story-of-the-hbgary-hack. 12 Alexandra Savelieva, Sergey Avdoshin.

24. Honan, M. (2012). *How Apple and Amazon security flaws led to my epic hacking*. Wired.com. http://www.wired.com/gadgetlab/2012/08/apple-amazon-mat-honan-hacking/
25. Honan, M. (2012). *How I resurrected my digital life after an epic hacking*. Wired.com. http://www.wired.com/gadgetlab/2012/08/mat-honan-data-recovery/
26. Russian Court Website Defaced in Support of Pussy Riot. (2012). Moscow: AFP. http://www.straitstimes.com/breaking-news/world/story/russian-court-website-defaced-support-pussy-riot-20120821
27. Rivner, U. (2011). *Anatomy of an attack*. Copyright 2011 EMC Corporation, http://blogs.rsa.com/anatomy-of-an-attack/
28. Tamai, T. (2009). Social impact of information system failures. *IEEE Computer, 42*(6), 58–65.
29. Avdoshin, S. M., Savelieva, A. A., & Serdiouk, V. A. (2010). *Microsoft technologies and products for information protection*. Microsoft Faculty Resource Center, https://www.facultyresourcecenter.com/curriculum/pfv.aspx?ID=8476&Login=
30. Kaspersky Lab Global Website. *IT security for the next generation*. http://www.kaspersky.com/about/events/educational-events/it_security_conference#tab=tab-4
31. Foundation for Educational Innovations. *Best proposals-2011*, http://www.hse.ru/org/hse/iff/methodics_2011

Industrial Internet Reference Architectures and Agent-Based Approach in Design and Manufacturing

Victor V. Taratukhin and Yulia V. Yadgarova

Abstract Multi-agent architecture allows us to develop decentralized and autonomous systems. This approach provides the flexibility and modularity but the problem appears to adapt and re-configuration of your system. In the context of Industry 4.0 [ISO/IEC/IEEE 42010:2011. Systems and software engineering -- Architecture description. [Internet]. Available from: http://www.iso.org/iso/catalogue_detail.htm?csnumber=50508] there are many examples of the complex behaviour of large systems which consist from agents. Agent-based approach for industrial internet architecture allows to perform complex behaviour and make predictions about how other components of the system will work. This paper provides an overview of some principles that can be used to develop multi-agent systems in case of Industrial Internet architecture.

Keywords Internet-of-things • Multi-agent systems • Industrial internet

1 Introduction

Nowadays, one of the main questions in developing an Industrial Internet [1] architecture is integration of business process management software and manufacturing field. Various architectures of manufacturing systems allow comparing these approaches and define the main principles of organization of such systems. The key problem of manufacturing architectures is changing environment and principles of organization of customer-oriented manufacturing process. Today most manufacturing architectures must support changing requirements. When we talk about customer-oriented manufacturing processes we mean that all products will be different from each other. The problem is to create agile manufacturing architecture to support full life-cycle of such production.

V.V. Taratukhin
ERCIS, University of Muenster, Münster, Germany

Y.V. Yadgarova (✉)
The Bauman Moscow State Technical University, Moskva, Russia
e-mail: y.v.yadgarova@gmail.com

© Springer International Publishing Switzerland 2016
J. Becker et al. (eds.), *Emerging Trends in Information Systems*, Progress in IS,
DOI 10.1007/978-3-319-23929-3_10

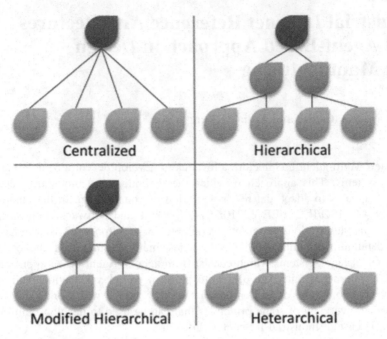

Fig. 1 Control architectures

Among various architectures of manufacturing systems it's possible to emphasize several main approaches of control systems. Historically production development starts from centralized architectures. The main types of such architectures are presented on Fig. 1 [2].

The centralized and hierarchical control architectures are characterized by single decision node (or several nodes) that perform core management functions. These architectures have a main disadvantage—when decision node breaks down the whole system loses the control. Another problem is the overall computation load on the control node. Such things make it impossible to develop agile architectures on the basis of centralized architectures.

Today in industrial automation systems prevailing a control model localized in scope and reactive in response, such as limited control loop and feedback mechanisms. This systems takes some inputs and produce some outputs (engineering data values) and control signals to hardware [3].

If we intend to perform distributed control, this control must be "intelligent and resilient", so that it can operate with a dynamic and unpredictable environment, using a distributed, collaborative capability to sense, make sense of and affect the world and so achieve the goals of the specific entry (agent) [4].

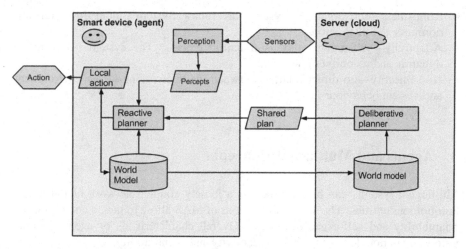

Fig. 2 Framework architecture

2   Decentralized Architectures

Traditional manufacturing control systems were developed when production processes were not such changeable. To cope with flexibility and reconfigurability of this environment decentralized architectures were developed.

Two main approaches of decentralized architectures are Multi-Agent Systems (MAS) [4] and Service Oriented Architecture (SOA) [5, 6].

SOA can be defined as

a set of architectural tenets for building autonomous yet interoperable systems [7].

SOA is based on the set of independent different modules available to interact with each other to perform user's task. Each service is autonomous and provides functionality that can be exposed by other services. This approach provides the ability to encapsulate complexity associated with manufacturing process. Similar to SOA, Multi-Agent systems can be described as a network of autonomous entities that perform social interactions and able to solve complex problems. Entities (agents) are adaptive to changes and naturally distributed. Thus, the high level of complexity of the system can be abstracted through coordination and cooperation of individual agents. Also multiagent systems often interact as bio-inspired and self-organized structures that achieve emergent behaviour of whole system.

Self-organization means that system has common characteristics:

• No explicit external control—system must be independent of external control unit.
• Global order from local interactions—ability to achieve global order through local interactions.
• Distributed control—in such systems control is distributed throughout the whole system. No central decision node is presented.

- Robustness—self-organized systems are robust. System should thrive on randomness and fluctuations.
- Adaptivity—self-organization is dynamic process. The system needs to be dynamic and reconfigurable.
- Non-linearity—no direct relation between the fluctuations of the environment and system behaviour [1].

3 Agents and Multiagent Concepts

Multiagent systems can be described as a loosely coupled network of individual autonomous entities. The social dimensions of MAS allow to tackle collaboration, adaptability and self-organization [8]. Overall characteristics of agents include autonomy, rationality, adaptability, reactivity and social-ability.

In the case of building decentralized Industrial Internet architecture in the scope of concrete agent there are mapped several properties:

- The relevant world model.
- Typical actions (both atomic and compound).
- Communication properties.
- Intension (as of other agents).
- Sensors.
- Actuation.
- Security [9].

4 Adaptive Multiagent Framework for Manufacturing Processes

As an example of multiagent decentralized architecture the overall functions of the intelligent control system in dynamic environment was presented. This architecture consists of several top-level decomposition modules, presented as follows:

Conceptual framework consists of several modules that are responsible for different functions.

Deliberative planner responsible for long-term plans of the system (deliberative). This plans are called *goals*. *Reactive planner* satisfying real-time decisions in accordance to deliberative plan. Short-horizon planner react to current situation and world model to execute concrete action.

The deliberative planner needs many resources to create plan and collect data from several devices (synchronize world model with local agents). Unlike the deliberative planner reactive planner has a strong connection with sensors and actuators and able to override actions with accordance to sensor information and world model.

The overall plan is not visible for any particular agent and observed by the remote service. Small and flexible reactive planner located on the device itself but long-term planner provided as a service in the cloud.

Another properties that has implemented by this model is security and safety. In the Industrial Internet architecture there are main capabilities of the system. So, the architecture includes another module that can be able to reject a request made by an operator and another agent. This module called *secure agent*. Secure agent also determine, when it is safe to change a device behavior.

Another part of the system provided by the most agent platforms is Yellow Page service [3] where agents should store meta-information to provide its capabilities to the community and describe them.

5 Interoperability and Composition with Other Production Services

The Industrial Internet architecture suggests interoperability and link between many diverse components from variety of vendors with different protocols. Distributed architecture are intended to be responsible to dynamic environment and resilient architectures need to adapt flexibly to optimize services as environment change.

This architecture require a flexible method of composing agents and services so that components can be dynamically integrated at run-time. Industrial Internet needs semantic interoperability to support many-to-many connections.

There are three main barriers with the interoperability of exchanging information:

- *Conceptual*—syntactic and semantic incompatibility
- *Technological*—incompatibility of IT architecture and platforms
- *Organizational*—incompatibility of organization structure and management techniques implemented in different enterprises.

According to this several interoperability concepts must be presented in the framework:

Interoperability of data—ability to operate together different data models which can locate on different machines with different operating systems.
Interoperability of services—refers to operate together different applications with syntactic and semantic differences
Interoperability of processes—aims to make various processes work together
Interoperability of business—refers to work in a harmonized way at the levels of organization and company

Practices and standards established today enabled constraint future capabilities, so approaches must provide tools for consuming re-evaluation and re-design the architecture.

6 Prototype Implementation

In this research, a prototype of the local control system which is capable of integrating with hardware devices is proposed. Such subsystem provides flexible configuration of each device. Rules of communication, ontology, knowledge base and facts base, each of these properties are configured separately by an engineer of corresponding domain.

The initial multi-agent system consists of different types of agents, group of agents and objects. In the designed subsystem the universal circuit board can be embedded in any device, controlled by a UNIX class operating system which contains an agent platform. The prototype implementation is presented at Fig. 3.

As a Smart device (agent), an implementation with RFID-readers to store real-time information about the product is used. Such information (destination, state and location of the part) influences the Cloud server.

For the purpose of efficiency increase of evolutionary search process it is necessary to develop and theoretically prove model of integration of subject-oriented analytical systems and genetic algorithms, for the purpose of an exception of unproductive branches of evolution. The subsequent inspection of the received models on adequacy can be made by development of multilevel neural network architecture of received systems models test.

Prototype of the control system consists of a single board computer, RFID reader and actuator. The scheme of the architecture is presented on Fig. 2. The single board

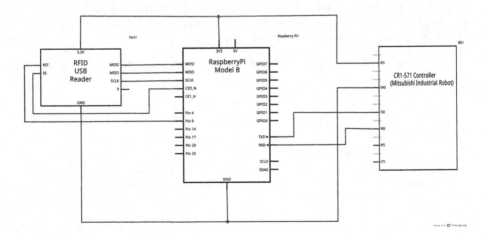

Fig. 3 Prototype implementation

computer holds UNIX OS on board and provides the software for controlling the agent, and power supply to the whole system.

The RFID reader is connected by means of SPI (Serial Peripheral Interface) interface via development board. This interface proves to be the most suitable for the kind of task, which the constructed device (the agent) fulfils. The interface can handle data speeds up to 10 Mbit/s. It works in full duplex mode. It also allows arbitrary choice of message size, content, and purpose. SPI is preferable for energy consumption factor as well, because in current design the device's peripherals don't use any outer power supply. Devices communicate in master/slave mode where the master device initiates the data frame. In the present design the Microcontroller of the single board computer plays a role of master device.

The exemplary executive device is Mitsubishi Industrial Robot (RV-1A Series). It is a compact 6-axis robot manipulator, which gives excellent options for build a flexible manufacturing system. You can see the device on Fig. 1. The robots controller supports RS-232 interface, so TxD and RxD pins of the single board computer are used to connect it.

After hardware connection there is a need to set a convenient software interface of communicating with RFID. The reader requires interface with registers and its native instructions. From the point of high-level code it's inconvenient. Another level of abstraction for communicating with RFID is needed. In order to control and interaction with RFID reader a 3-rd party Python library is used. Python allows importing GPIO and SPI wrapper. It hides low level abstractions and provides quite a convenient interface of communication with RFID. It operates 64 registers of the RFID -device and uses native instructions, common for SPI interaction. Functions of software:

- Reading part's data and store current information of its state.
- Update data during processing
- Communication with other agents.

7   Conclusions

This paper provides an overview of some of the principles in building Industrial Internet architectures that we can use to develop multi-agent systems to solve problems in the field of production process. As an exemplary framework, including distributed control system based on multiagent technologies is presented.

Semantic approach to communication between agents allows increase interoperability and communication both between enterprises as between information parts in the enterprise.

Prototype of the system is developed. This model is applicable to work with various manufacturing agents in conjunction with different design agents and control systems.

References

1. ISO/IEC/IEEE 42010:2011. *Systems and software engineering -- Architecture description.* [Internet]. Available from: http://www.iso.org/iso/catalogue_detail.htm?csnumber=50508
2. João, D. F. (2013). *Bio-inspired self-organisation in evolvable production systems* [Internet]. Available from: http://www.diva-portal.org/smash/get/diva2:652487/FULLTEXT02\
3. Industrial Internet Consortium. [Internet]. 2015 [cited May 28, 2015]. Available from: https://workspace.iiconsortium.org/kws/groups/tech/download.php/818/Industrial%20I nternet%20Vocabulary%201.0.pdf
4. Wooldridge, M. (2009). *An introduction to multiagent systems.* New York: Wiley.
5. Monostori, L., Vancza, J., & Kumara, S. R. T. (2006). Agent-based systems for manufacturing. *CIRP Annals-Manufacturing Technology, 55*(2), 697–720.
6. Semantic SOA Makes Sense. [Internet]. Available from: http://enterpriseweb.com/semantic-soa-makes-sense-2/
7. Jammes, F., et al. (2005). *Orchestration of service-oriented manufacturing processes. Distributed data mining: An overview.* IEEE TCDP newsletter.
8. Taratoukhine, V., & Bechkoum, K. (1999). Towards a consistent distributed design: A multi-agent approach. In *Proceedings of IEEE information visualization'99.*
9. Functional Safety. [Internet]. Available from: http://www.iec.ch/functionalsafety/explained/.

Cloud-Based Engineering Design
and Manufacturing: A Survey

E. Tarchinskaya, V. Taratukhin, and J. Becker

Abstract This paper presents a literature research and semi-structured web-based survey on what changes and concepts are needed and posed by the requirements and challenges in manufacturing, and how cloud computing may help to meet those requirements and realize them in manufacturing operations. In this contribution, we outline the primary discussed in the academia manufacturing paradigm, as well as we derive a number of business requirements this paradigm poses on the current manufacturing business model. With the help of empirical survey, we try then to identify whether new technology in the form of the cloud computing concept can help to change the way companies operate in the manufacturing industry and meet the requirements of a new manufacturing paradigm.

Keywords Manufacturing • Engineering design • Cloud computing • Agile manufacturing • Business processes

1   Introduction

According to the largest software vendors' observation, leading manufacturers in order to develop the most satisfying product delivering a greater value to the customer have to maintain a closer collaboration throughout the entire value chain [1, 2]. This is explained by the fact that manufacturing industry is recently experiencing various challenges related to rapidly changing markets, globalization, increased global competition, demanding customers seeking complex, diverse, and at same time low cost products [3, 4].

Both practitioners and academics agree that these newly appeared challenges require new patterns of production organization, more dynamic and flexible, which can adapt easily to the changes occurring in the environment [5]. One of largest

E. Tarchinskaya (✉)
Bauman Moscow State Technical University, ul. Baumanskaya 2-ya, 5, 105005 Moscow, Russia
e-mail: k.tarchinskaya@gmail.com

V. Taratukhin • J. Becker
University of Münster, Leonardo-Campus, 48149 Münster, Germany
e-mail: victor.taratoukhine@ercis.uni-muenster.de; becker@ercis.uni-muenster.de

© Springer International Publishing Switzerland 2016
J. Becker et al. (eds.), *Emerging Trends in Information Systems*, Progress in IS,
DOI 10.1007/978-3-319-23929-3_11

software vendors emphasizes that integrated product development is a key factor to success for manufacturers to prosper in the modern reality [1]. Collaborative design process including close cooperation of product designers with other teams in the value chain as well as continuous alignment with the end customer, according to the same vendor, improves and enables: better product manufacturability, logistics, better decision making, change management processes, reuse of components, and continuous product transformation [1, 2].

However, advances in IT and, in particular, the emergence of the cloud computing concept can give organizations opportunities to become more information-oriented, knowledge-driven, and automate much of their daily operations around the global information network [6]. The trend of the cloud is on the wave of software vendors' discussions stating that this technology is able to "...*increase their [manufacturers'] participation in solution-provider networks by providing integrated business processes across a single organization or spread throughout several enterprises in multiple industries*" [1]. As a result, cloud-based technologies slowly penetrate the manufacturing industry. Several computer aided design (CAD) vendors, such as Ascon Group[1] and Autodesk,[2] have already announced offering their CAD software in the cloud. Nevertheless, as the market and the understanding of cloud computing grows, the drivers and deployment scenarios that framed the initial cloud agenda are becoming increasingly irrelevant. Today companies expect benefits that go way beyond cost savings and efficiency and are starting to focus increasingly on cloud solutions that facilitate business innovation and growth [7]. Thereby, the move to the cloud requires a more careful analysis of which areas would benefit from the cloud, and close attention to inevitable changes that will result in the organization.

In this paper, we continue exploring the research started in our previous papers: Tarchinskaya et al. [8] and Tarchinskaya et al. [9]. We make stress on the cloud computing concept and continue to analyse how new manufacturing methodologies and the cloud computing concept might be aligned and mitigate stated challenges in manufacturing. In our previous papers, we reported a literature review to address this motivation. However, in this work, we attempt to show a broader overview of the research, and, thereby, opinions of the practitioners will be counted in the form of web-based survey study.

The purpose in undertaking and further developing such a research is threefold. The first aim is to deliver insights into current state and area of improvement in the manufacturing industry and investigate how innovation technologies can be applied there. Secondly, based on the obtained information this paper intends to raise the number of implications and questions about the applicability of cloud-based technologies in manufacturing industry. The third aim is to stimulate the future research and debate devoted to the cloud computing concept, its implementation in manufacturing industry, and industry requirements.

---

[1] http://ascon.net/main/

[2] http://www.autodesk.com/

Hence, the reminder of the paper is structured as follows. First, we will give a short summary of previous conducted theoretical base. Afterwards, we will proceed with the structure and results of the web-based survey. At the end, we will conclude with a summary and a research outlook.

2 Literature Review

As mentioned above, most of described literature review was elaborated in detail in our previous papers by Tarchinskaya et al. [8, 9]. To avoid repetition, we would like to state only the overall literature review methodology and the digest of the main research findings served as the ground for our web-based survey.

2.1 Methodology

The literature review is based on the research method presented by Webster and Watson [10]. The main focus of the review lies on journal and conference publications due to their high quality and timeliness, and ScienceDirect[3] database was chosen as a starting point for the analysis. Extending the time frame to the maximum and without limitation to the source, the goal to cover a broad range of relevant literature was achieved. To capture articles dealing with the latest requirements, challenges, and trends in the manufacturing industry, we searched for different combinations of phrases including the terms "web-based/service-based/multi-agent/agent-based/agile" and "engineering de-sign/manufacturing" in the title, abstract, and keywords. In the selected time frame and from all search queries, 81 candidate articles were chosen by reading abstracts of the papers. After going through a full-text search, among these 81 articles 41 papers were selected and deemed as the most relevant for the literature review. Based on the candidate articles found through the initial review, forward and backward searches were conducted to identify additional articles. Regarding the backward search, further contributions were included by analysing references of the initial papers which were relevant for our context. Overall, after performing backward search additional 10 articles were gathered. Concerning the forward search, Google Scholar[4] and databases in which the article was founded for citations of the respective papers were checked. As a result of the forward search, 24 more papers were obtained. Eventually, the basis of the literature review was grounded on 75 articles.

---

[3] http://www.sciencedirect.com/

[4] https://scholar.google.ru/

2.2 A Condensed Summary of Literature Review Findings

Based on the theoretical foundation of 75 articles, we identified that the concept of agile manufacturing is proliferating one in academic discussions related to the search of new paradigms for manufacturing. Moreover, in the previous works, a definition of agile manufacturing paradigm according to three levels of granularity was extracted. Thus, a company that wants to achieve excellence in one or several of these areas, first of all, needs to understand the meaning of the agile manufacturing paradigm on three different levels: *strategic, tactical,* and *operational*:

On a strategic level, the paradigm refers to the ability of an entire company to open up new markets, develop products and services in great demand with respect to changing customer needs [11]. The strategic level also denotes an enterprise's ability to join and leave various production networks [12], according to the company's current needs, and to extend or reduce the number of network members depending on the needed competencies for developing, producing, and marketing a product.

On a tactical level, agile manufacturing refers to the ability of an entire manufacturing enterprise to make changes to its product portfolio, and to move, e.g. to other product families, if needed, and produce them quickly [11].

On an operational level, the paradigm refers to the ability of a manufacturing or assembly system, of a single machine or of a group of machines to switch to a particular family of work pieces through removal or addition of functional elements [11], which allows to flexibly adjust production capacities on a daily basis.

Having identified a major concept, we attempted to derive from the academic literature business requirements imposed to current manufacturing business model by newly appeared manufacturing concept and current market environment. Therefore, the literature review identified ten generic business requirements imposed by the agile manufacturing concept and formulated as follows in Table 1 [8, 9]:

Thus, the analysis of the literature shows that manufacturing companies have to be re-structured or re-organized in order to overcome challenges of the twenty-first century, where there are customers who have highly specific and rapidly changing needs, global networking, migration and physical distribution of manufacturing facilities, etc. [27, 30]. Manufacturers have to respond to these needs in a new, fast, and uncertain environment with suitable products and services to survive in the competition. Described situation imposes a number of new requirements which dictate companies how they are supposed to behave. The backbone of these requirements is the ability to work in globally dispersed, temporary networks of manufacturing participants with core competences. On top of that, product development is recognized now as a key process of competition which effective and efficient management is vital. To counter these challenges and new requirements, a new manufacturing paradigm has emerged. This paradigm is called by unique term—agile manufacturing. Agile manufacturing demands advances in information

Table 1 Generic business requirements

R#	Description	Article
R1.	Strong focus on core competencies and core business processes of the organization	[13]
R2.	Rapid team formation	[14]
R3.	Concurrent activities of manufacturing and product design processes	[12, 14, 15]
R4.	Communication and collaborative work among multiple actors along value chain	[13, 14, 16–22]
R5.	Communication and collaborative work among multiple actors in product development and design groups	[14, 22–26]
R6.	Data exchange among multiple actors along the entire value chain	[15, 20, 21, 27, 28]
R7.	Data integration	[20, 29]
R8.	Immediate access to the data	[20]
R9.	Remote access to the data	[15, 20]
R10.	IT integration	[12, 19, 25, 27]

technology. IT and physical tools are inevitable for the support of agile manufacturing paradigm and play a great role in realizing required integration and collaboration in new generation manufacturing [4, 12, 27].

3 Integration of Manufacturing Paradigms with the Cloud

To show a broader overview of this research, opinions of the practitioners will be counted in the form of web-based survey study.

3.1 Web-Based Survey Methodology

Literature research revealed the number of agile manufacturing requirements. The initial goal of the semi-structured survey is to confirm the actuality of agile manufacturing requirements found during the literature research, to collect new requirements, if any, and, most importantly, collect experts' thoughts regarding whether or not they consider the implementation of cloud computing technologies in manufacturing as a possible remedy or solution to meet those requirements.

Regarding the design of the very content of the questionnaire, it was mainly based on the results from the literature review. A particular approach of the questionnaire is to fulfil the survey goal defined and thus to explore the knowledge of the survey participants. In this sense, the first questions are the open questions and serve to gather opinions about the cloud computing. Then, a special attention of the questionnaire is drawn toward the confirmation of literature findings by experts.

At the end, the survey sets the questions devoted to the correlation of the cloud and agile manufacturing requirements.

To provide the best possible and global pool of experts, two main groups of experts were targeted: professionals and experts in the sphere of information technologies and/or professionals from the manufacturing industry working at SAP SE.[5] Approximately near to 70 potential participants were either informed to access the questionnaire or contacted directly. At the end, a little bit more that 50 % of targeted respondents kindly answered the questions of the survey.

3.2 Web-Based Survey Results

General opinion about cloud computing. This section of the web-based survey consisted of the open questions targeted at collecting the understanding of participants regarding cloud computing as a whole and its applicability in manufacturing. The results of this section are the following.

Question 1: Do you think that cloud computing technologies can be adopted and widely used in manufacturing?

82 % of respondents had a consensus that cloud computing technologies can be adopted and widely used in manufacturing industry. Only 6 % of participants expressed explicitly negative opinion on this matter and responded that cloud computing cannot be beneficial to manufacturing. Some answers elaborated on this question and stated that cloud computing can be used, for example, to establish e-Procurement and e-Commerce platforms, to have an access to servers and data storages, to put in the cloud commodity type services (e.g. Sharepoint, e-mail), and to support mobile technologies.

Question 2: Do you think that cloud computing technologies are able to yield benefits for the manufacturing industry? If yes, in what way?

12 % of survey participants responded "no" to this question. Other answers varied in statements of the benefits of cloud computing for manufacturing. According to survey responses, cloud computing technologies provide a potential to access real-time manufacturing information from any device and, as a result, enable mobility. From this perspective, the cloud can support real-time operations and fast data processing as well as improve IT data management. Among other benefits, participants of the survey also mentioned that cloud computing technologies are able to improve the integration of supply chains and various participants of manufacturing process through the utilization of such technologies as SaaS and PaaS, for instance. On top of that, many responses were related to the benefits of cost savings. Thus, according to the survey opinion, with cloud computing technologies manufacturing companies, especially small- and medium-sized ones, can

---

[5] http://www.sap.com/corporate-en/about.html

reduce costs on investments in hardware and "in-house" software solutions. In this sense, the cost can be saved by putting commodity type of services into the cloud. Yet another important aspect mentioned in the participants' answers was that the cloud computing technologies have a power to enhance flexibility of the manufacturing organization. First of all, cloud technologies give an opportunity to better respond to market changes as the company can access needed software and services via the cloud which it does not have in-house. Second of all, the cloud computing technologies allow the computing infrastructure dynamically grow or shrink according to the current demands (e.g. according to the volume of production) of the company.

Question 3: Do you think that cloud computing technologies are able to alter manufacturing business processes and enhance them? If yes, in what way?

23 % of responses stated that cloud computing technologies are not able to completely affect and/or alter manufacturing processes. With the introduction of cloud computing technologies may simplify some processes by the automation of some process steps and in the workflow. Also some processes might become less dependent on some specific location. Furthermore, many responses acknowledge the fact that cloud computing technologies may enhance the integration with vendors, customers, and the underlying logistics process by providing alternative ways of communication and collaboration as well as possibility to have global MRP/ERP system. Consequently, the integration and collaboration between business partners will be faster and more efficient.

New requirements for the manufacturing industry. This section of the survey questionnaire intends to gather opinions about agile manufacturing requirements found during literature review. For this reason, the requirements detected in the literature review were concisely formulated in the form of semi-structured questions. Thus, the participant of the web-based survey were asked to grade the validity of the given statements on the Likert scale (ranging from 1 to 5, where 1 corresponds with completely disagree and where 5 corresponds with completely agree), or to insert the comments in special cases. Likert scale was used in order to show the general opinion and impressions regarding the variety of agile manufacturing requirements. At this point, the option of having different statements graded equally high (or low) was not a threat, but rather an indicator of a real practitioners' opinion on this matter (Table 2).

Overall, according to the survey answers, questions 1 and 6 in this section proofs the requirements concurrency of activities and close collaboration. Question 2 is concerned with the requirement rapid team formation. The responses to question 3 confirm the actuality of new requirement data exchange among multiple actors along the entire supply chain. The ratings of question 5 proof the requirement IT integration.

Question 4 is related to efficient information networking and what aspects of it are deemed the most important for the manufacturing industry. Most participants agree that information integration from various machines, remote access, and immediate, real-time access to the data is necessary in manufacturing.

Table 2 Questions about new requirements

#	Questions	Correlation of answers according to Likert scale
1	Agile manufacturing requires a close communication and collaborative work: (a) among manufacturers, suppliers, customers, and product development teams; (b) within product development team	(a) 4.47 (b) 4.47
2	The challenges of modern market imply manufacturers to follow the concept of rapid team formation where independent organizations form temporary alliances in order to capitalize on core competences and achieve collaborative production	4.06
3	There is a need for the establishment of efficient information networking	4.59
4	Efficient information networking in the context of the previous question incorporates: (a) information integration from various machines; (b) remote access to the data; (c) immediate, real-time access to the data	(a) 4.12 (b) 4.61 (c) 4.89
5	Future operations in manufacturing organizations will require the integration of information systems through scattered manufacturing plants	4.29
6	Design has to become a concurrent and holistic production process	4

Correlation of the cloud computing and agile manufacturing requirements for the manufacturing industry. While previous section of questions in the survey intends to confirm agile manufacturing requirements, this section aims at collecting opinions regarding whether or not cloud computing technologies are able to meet those requirements. Therefore, the Likert scale was used again in order to grade statements about the correlation of cloud computing capabilities with regard to the manufacturing industry (Table 3).

The agreement of survey participants concerning the ability of the cloud to satisfy manufacturing requirement is less strong. The average value of agreement for this area is 3.82 what is positioned between "Agree" and "Neutral". It is evident that cloud computing technologies are not fully accepted in the context of manufacturing industry among professionals and experts. The most agreement participants reached in the statement that cloud computing can enable efficient information networking. The least agreement was gained in the sphere of concurrent product development and design.

Likewise in previous section, question 4 is related to efficient information networking and what aspects of it cloud computing technologies can support. Most participants agree that information integration from various machines, remote access, and immediate, real-time access to the data can be enabled by the cloud. However, there is no ultimate agreement among the web-based survey participants.

Table 3 Questions about cloud computing and new requirements

#	Questions	Correlation of answers according to Likert scale
1	The cloud computing technologies in manufacturing have a power to enable close communication and collaborative work: (a) among manufacturers, suppliers, customers, and product development teams; (b) within product development team	(a) 3.88 (b) 3.88
2	The cloud computing technologies can support the concept of rapid team formation	3.76
3	The cloud computing technologies are able to contribute to the establishment of efficient information networking	4.06
4	The cloud computing technologies are able to provide: (a) information integration from various machines; (b) remote access to the data; (c) immediate, real-time access to the data	(a) 3.87 (b) 4.33 (c) 4.33
5	The cloud computing technologies have a power to enable the integration of information systems through scattered manufacturing plants	4
6	The cloud computing technologies can support and enable concurrent product development and design	3.5

3.3 Assessment of Empirical Results

The conclusions related to the web-based survey results can be summed up in the following structured list:

First of all, the survey results confirm the actuality of agile manufacturing requirements identified in the literature review. The overall opinion of survey participants states that cloud computing technologies have the ability to support, optimize, and alter manufacturing processes in order to meet agile manufacturing requirements. This can be concluded by the general statistics of answers to questions related to the identification of cloud computing abilities to fulfil certain agile manufacturing requirement.

The web-based survey results showed that cloud computing technologies are deemed to be able: (1) to enhance the integration with vendors, customers, and the underlying logistics processes; (2) to provide common IT infrastructure to all members of manufacturing process. Therefore, cloud computing is capable of providing integration what is identified as one of the agile manufacturing components.

The results also showed that such cloud computing enabled integration provides new ways of communication among manufacturing business partners and makes collaboration more efficient. Hence, it corresponds to the second agile manufacturing characteristic—collaboration.

Furthermore, the survey participants acknowledged the fact that cloud computing technologies applied in the manufacturing industry are able to enhance the flexibility of manufacturing process. Cloud computing can improve the overall enterprise flexibility by: (1) providing the opportunity to access needed IT infrastructure which is not in-house via the cloud; (2) allowing the computing infrastructure dynamically grow or shrink; (3) reducing costs on IT investments.

4 Summary

Following the research motivation, this paper provides insights into challenges imposed on the manufacturing industry. Firstly, it identifies and provides a structured view of new paradigm emerged in the manufacturing industry—agile manufacturing, multilevel meaning of agile manufacturing paradigm, and its business requirements imposed to enterprises operating in the manufacturing industry. Secondly, cloud computing is argued as a promising concept that might enable agile manufacturing and enhance existing business model of the manufacturing industry. This paper represents only first results in the research area of potential applicability of cloud computing technologies in manufacturing processes. Thus, the literature review findings together with empirical research represent the foundation and guidance for future research on applicability of cloud-based technologies in the manufacturing industry and their interconnection with agile manufacturing paradigm.

References

1. SAP SE. (2013). *Integrated product development.* Available at: http://www.sap.com/bin/sapcom/en_us/downloadasset.2013-05-may-07-11.solution-in-detail-industrial-machinery-and-components-integrated-product-development-pdf.bypassReg.html
2. SAP SE. (2012). *Powering a solution provider network.* Available at http://www.sap.com/bin/sapcom/en_us/downloadasset.2012-12-dec-27-09.industry-executive-overview-industrial-machinery-and-components-powering-a-solution-provider-network-pdf.bypassReg.html
3. Gunasekaran, A. (1999). Agile manufacturing: A framework for research and development. *International Journal of Production Economics, 62*(1–2), 87–105.
4. Tian, G., Yin, G., & Taylor, D. (2002). Internet-based manufacturing: A review and a new infrastructure for distributed intelligent manufacturing. *Journal of Intelligent Manufacturing, 13*, 323–338.
5. Macia-Perez, F., et al. (2012). Cloud agile manufacturing. *IOSR Journal of Engineering, 2*(5), 1045–1048.
6. Rahman, S. M., Sarker, R., & Bignall, B. (1999). Application of multimedia technology in manufacturing: A review. *Computers in Industry, 38*(1), 43–52.
7. Kisker, H. (2012). *The changing cloud agenda* (pp. 1–19). Forrester Research, Inc.
8. Tarchinskaya, E., Taratoukhine, V., & Matzner, M. (2013). Cloud-based engineering design and manufacturing: State-of-the-art. In *Proceedings of the 2013 IFAC conference on manufacturing, modelling, management, and control (IFAC MIM 2013)* (pp. 353–358). St. Petersburg, Russian Federation.

9. Tarchinskaya, E., Taratoukhine, V., & Becker, J. (2014). Exploring application of cloud computing concept to new paradigms in manufacturing. In H. Krcmar & K. Turowski (Eds.), *Very large business applications (VLBA)* (pp. 39–47). Aachen: Shaker.
10. Watson, R. T., & Webster, J. (2002). Analyzing the past to prepare for the future: writing a literature review. *MIS Quarterly, 26*(2), xiii–xxiii.
11. Wiendahl, H.-P., et al. (2007). Changeable manufacturing - classification, design and operation. *CIRP Annals Manufacturing Technology, 56*(2), 783–809.
12. Gunasekaran, A., McGaughey, R., & Wolstencroft, V. (2001). Agile manufacturing: Concepts and framework. In *Agile Manufacturing: The 21st Century Competitive Strategy* (pp. 26–49).
13. Taylor, P., Jagdev, H. S., & Browne, J. (2010). The extended enterprise-a context for manufacturing. *Production Planning & Control: The Management of Operations, 9*(3), 216–229.
14. Subba Rao, S., & Nahm, A. (2001). *Information systems for agile manufacturing environment in the post-industrial stage* (pp. 229–246).
15. Eynard, B. (2005). Web-based collaborative engineering support system: Applications in mechanical design and structural analysis. *Concurrent Engineering, 13*(2), 145–153.
16. Baker, A. D. (1999). Agents and the internet: Infrastructure for mass customization. *IEEE Internet Computing*, (October), 62–69.
17. Bouzakis, K.-D., et al. (2009). Automating the manufacturing process under a web based framework. *Advances in Engineering Software, 40*(9), 956–964.
18. Camarinha-Matos, L. M., & Afsarmanesh, H. (1998). Towards an architecture for virtual enterprises. *Journal of Intelligent Manufacturing, 9*, 189–199.
19. Coronado, A. E., Sarhadi, M., & Millar, C. (2002). Defining a framework for information systems requirements for agile manufacturing. *International Journal of Production Economics, 75*(1–2), 57–68.
20. Cheng, K., & Bateman, R. J. (2008). E-manufacturing: Characteristics, applications and potentials. *Progress in Natural Science, 18*(11), 1323–1328.
21. Smparounis, K. (2011). A Web-based platform for collaborative product design and evaluation. *Mechanical Engineering*, 35–56.
22. Weston, R. H., Harrison, R., & West, A. A. (2007). Virtual enterprise engineering in support of distributed and agile manufacture. In *Agile manufacturing: The 21st century competitive strategy* (pp. 703–734). Amsterdam: Elsevier. doi:10.1016/B978-008043567-1/50036-X.
23. Fuh, J. Y. H., & Li, W. D. (2005). Advances in collaborative CAD: The-state-of-the art. *Computer-Aided Design, 37*(5), 571–581.
24. Gunasekaran, A., & Love, P. E. (1999). A review of multimedia technology in manufacturing. *Computers in Industry, 38*(1), 65–76. Available at: http://linkinghub.elsevier.com/retrieve/pii/S0166361598001080.
25. Hao, Q., et al. (2006). Agent-based collaborative product design engineering: An industrial case study. *Computers in Industry, 57*(1), 26–38. Available at: http://linkinghub.elsevier.com/retrieve/pii/S0166361505001405. Accessed September 20, 2012.
26. Lees, B., Branki, C., & Aird, I. (2001). A framework for distributed agent-based engineering design support. *Automation in Construction, 10*(5), 631–637.
27. Büyüközkan, G., Dereli, T., & Baykasoglu, A. (2004). A survey on the methods and tools of concurrent new product development and agile manufacturing. *Journal of Intelligent Manufacturing, 15*, 731–751.
28. Guerra, M. A. P., & Zhang, W. Z. (2001). Computer applications in agile manufacturing. *Agile Manufacturing: The 21st Century Competitive Strategy, 1988*, 317–336.
29. Saha, R., & Grover, S. (2011). Identifying enablers of e-manufacturing. *ISRN Mechanical Engineering, 2011*, 1–6.
30. Westkämper, E. (2007). Digital manufacturing in the global era. *Digital Enterprise Technology*, 1–11.

Printed in the United States
By Bookmasters